a year of
READING

a year of
READING

A MONTH-BY-MONTH GUIDE TO CLASSICS AND CROWD-PLEASERS FOR YOU OR YOUR BOOK GROUP

ELISABETH ELLINGTON, PhD & JANE FREIMILLER, PhD

sourcebooks

Published by Sourcebooks, Inc.
P.O. Box 4410, Naperville, Illinois 60567-4410
(630) 961-3900
Fax: (630) 961-2168
www.sourcebooks.com

Originally published in 2002 by Sourcebooks, Inc.

Library of Congress Cataloging-in-Publication Data is on file with the publisher.

Printed and bound in the United States of America.
WOZ 10 9 8 7 6 5 4 3 2 1

CLASSIC ROMANCE
THIS DIGITAL LIFE
CREATIVE SPIRIT

FAMILIES IN FICTION
JOURNEYS

TABLE OF CONTENTS

~ INTRODUCTION ~

How to Make This Year
Your Best Year of Reading Ever

"When I get a little money I buy books; and if any is left I buy food and clothes."

—ERASMUS (CA. 1466–1536)

People who are passionate about reading do not have to be convinced of its benefits. We know that reading opens our minds, challenges our beliefs, and expands our hearts. Books are there for us whether we're celebrating or mourning. We bond with people over books, though we may have nothing else in common. Passionate readers easily agree with Erasmus in ranking books as foremost among the necessities of life.

But even committed readers run into problems. Which among the thousands of books published each year are worth reading? How can we navigate a course through all the millions of books available? How can we think more deeply about the reading choices we make? Wouldn't it be great to structure our choices in ways that build on and complement one another?

A Year of Reading is designed to help you see your way clearly through the myriad of choices available. In addition to suggesting books, we provide questions for thinking about what you've read. Sprinkled throughout the book are film recommendations, facts about authors and topics, and activities for book clubs. There are lots of ideas here, so readers and groups can pick and choose what works best for them.

For readers interested in starting a book group or improving the one they're in, information in the back of the book covers the basics, from finding other members to choosing a meeting place, as well as more complex issues such as managing group dynamics and a variety of suggestions for making meetings more engaging and enjoyable.

Finally, we would love to hear about your reading. What books and advice would you give to other readers? Which of our suggestions worked well for you? Email us at yearofreading2017@gmail.com, look for us on social media, and let us know about your reading!

⚘ LET'S GET STARTED ⚘

Make a plan. What do you want to accomplish with your reading this year? Finally read Charles Dickens? Learn some world history? Spend some time reflecting on what you loved about your reading life last year and how you might build on that this year. Consider, too, where your reading life fell short. Set goals!

Join a challenge. Google "reading challenges for adults" and you won't be disappointed. Some of our favorites include:

- Read more women authors. Books by women are still underrepresented among prestigious review sites and literary prizes.

- Read authors of color. Books by authors of color are definitely underrepresented on the bestseller lists too!

- Read harder books. Challenge yourself to read books that are long or seem difficult. You may be pleasantly surprised at how much you enjoy them.

- Read your own damn books. Pick up books you already own but haven't had time to read yet.

- Read banned books. Somewhere, someone is banning a great book. Find out what those books are and support freedom of speech by reading them.

Track your reading. Keep a list of what you've read and what you want to read. Maybe add a mini-review or rating to remind yourself what you thought. We like to track our reading online at Goodreads.com, where you can build shelves for your books, rate books, post and read reviews, and join reading groups. LibraryThing.com and Shelfari.com are two more social media websites that allow you to track and organize your reading and connect with other readers.

Keep a reading journal. Many readers use writing to deepen their understanding of books. We read with a notebook nearby for taking notes, copying quotations we like, and writing down titles of books we'd like to read next. Consider making entries as you read. You'll find many lists of excellent reading journal questions online, but we can usually push ourselves to think more deeply simply by focusing on basic questions: What do you like about the book so far? Dislike? What surprises you? What puzzles you?

Start a book blog. In under five minutes, your new book blog could be up and running. Wordpress and Blogger are two websites where you can sign up for a free blog. Post reviews of what you read, or participate in different weekly book blogging memes. You'll find a master list of popular book blogging memes at girlxoxo.com. Or search for three of our favorites:

- *It's Monday! What Are You Reading?* Share what you've been reading and what you plan to read next.
- *Top Ten Tuesday.* Create a weekly top-ten book list on different themes.
- *Friday Finds.* Post your best book finds of the week.

Read more award-winning books. Even when we don't agree that a book deserves the award, we enjoy the debate. Some awards, such as the National Book Award and the Man Booker Prize, release long lists and short lists well in advance of the award announcement, which gives readers time to read the nominated books and be prepared with informed opinions.

Read outside your comfort zone. Challenges are great, but if you set yourself a challenge, make sure it is not simply a numerical one. If you're skittish about poetry, give it a try. Are you sure you hate science fiction? We've put some accessible sci-fi titles in this book. We've also included a number of graphic novels and young adult (YA) books here, which we are convinced you will adore once you give them a try.

Find a real-world community. As much as we love the Internet, we think nothing takes the place of getting together with other people and talking about books in person. If you're not already part of a book club, check with your local library, bookstores, continuing education programs, or community centers to find one. Or start one yourself! See our suggestions in the back of this book for how to do that.

Join the conversation. Many authors are active on social media sites like Twitter, Facebook, and Instagram. Many also have active websites and blogs. Follow authors on Twitter and like their pages on Facebook. Find out when and where they are giving readings. Find out what interests they have and what books they are recommending.

Attend a reading or a book festival. Start small with an author appearance at your local library or bookstore. When you travel, check local listings for readings and festivals. Many colleges and universities sponsor readings and book festivals. For the truly ambitious, consider attending an event like Book Riot Live or BookExpo America.

Read locally. Is your town or city known for a particular author or authors? Check with your local library if you're not sure. Many authors' homes have been turned into museums. Perhaps there's one near you. If you live in a university town, there could be an author or two in the literature department. Look them up.

Read internationally. We've included some books that do not take place in the U.S. by authors who aren't American. Check out

In the Land of Invisible Women in our July chapter, or *Please Look After Mom* and *Under the Udala Trees*, both in May. The change in perspective is fascinating. Once you get started, you will want more. Consider picking one country each year to explore through reading.

Think like an author. You've done a lot of reading. Isn't it time to maybe, just maybe, put your pen to paper and start writing? Consider signing up for a writing challenge. We like NaNoWriMo, National Novel Writing Month: during the month of November, hundreds of thousands of people commit to writing a 50,000-word novel. NaPoWriMo is a daily poetry challenge for March. Another thirty-day challenge that you could do any month is the Writing Prompt 30-Day Challenge.

Be guided by serendipity. Yes, we know, this is the opposite of everything we just said. But sometimes, someone on a bus will be engrossed in a book and you have to know what it is. Sometimes, train stations have bookshelves of donated texts and one catches your eye. Other times, there is a title you just can't get out of your head. Do not ignore these impulses—go for it!

A HAPPIER YOU

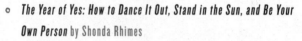

- *The Year of Yes: How to Dance It Out, Stand in the Sun, and Be Your Own Person* by Shonda Rhimes
- *Stumbling on Happiness* by Daniel Gilbert
- *Felicity: Poems* by Mary Oliver
- *The Principles of Uncertainty* by Maira Kalman
- *Happy All the Time* by Laurie Colwin

January inspires us to take stock of our lives and make plans for the future. The weather conspires to keep us inside, giving us the opportunity for self-study. We owe it to ourselves to spend some time thinking about where we are, how we got here, and where we are going. This month's selections are all inspired by the introspection winter brings, and the renewed hope for happiness that comes with each new year.

THE YEAR OF YES: HOW TO DANCE IT OUT, STAND IN THE SUN, AND BE YOUR OWN PERSON

Shonda Rhimes

You may find yourself wondering just how Shonda Rhimes does it. She is a single mother with three daughters, and as the writer-producer of *Grey's Anatomy*, *Scandal*, and *How to Get Away with Murder*, she owns Thursday night television. It's a breathtaking juggling act, as she reminds us many times in *The Year of Yes*, her memoir of a yearlong experiment in saying yes to opportunity, to herself, and, ultimately, to happiness.

What was the secret to Rhimes's success? She said no. To everything. And while saying no freed her up to focus on her career and motherhood, it meant that she missed out on opportunities to be happier and more engaged in life. An under-her-breath complaint by her older sister ("You never say yes to anything") launches Rhimes into a crisis of self-doubt and self-questioning leading to the realization that even though she "has it all," whatever that means, she's deeply unhappy. Her solution? Say yes.

Reading *The Year of Yes* is like sitting down for a visit with your best girlfriend, the one who can spin a good story out of anything, who makes you laugh until your sides ache, whose thoughtful advice you seek when you have a problem. Much of this book is very funny, and Rhimes is never afraid to turn a sharply critical eye on herself and her own flaws and foibles. The opportunities to which Rhimes says yes—delivering the commencement speech at Dartmouth College, appearing on *Jimmy Kimmel Live*—are not likely to be the same kinds of invitations you and I might receive, but there is much to learn from Rhimes's life lessons and wisdom. Ultimately, this is a book about being present in the moment, reframing challenges, living courageously, and loving yourself.

DISCUSSION/REFLECTION STRATEGIES

- One of the most rewarding yeses for Rhimes is saying yes to play, and she discovers that time with her children is her "happy place." What is your happy place? Rhimes finds she needs to spend only fifteen minutes playing with her daughters to feel recharged. If you had fifteen minutes a day to spend on yourself, what would you spend it doing?

Did You Know...?

Shonda Rhimes was profiled in the PBS series *Makers: Women Who Make America* as one of the most influential women in Hollywood. The series, a follow-up to the 2013 documentary of the same name, looks at the lives of women breaking ground in different walks of life.

EXTRA CREDIT

Memoirs of yearlong experiments in self-improvement are so popular that they are virtually a subcategory in the field of self-help books. A good place to start further exploration is Gretchen Rubin's *The Happiness Project*, an engagingly written account of Rubin's research into the science and philosophy of happiness and month-by-month attempts to become happier. A. J. Jacobs has turned the yearlong experiment into his life's work: look for *The Know-It-All: One Man's Humble Quest to Become the Smartest Person in the World* and *Drop Dead Healthy: One Man's Humble Quest for Bodily Perfection*. For a balanced look at the rewards and potential downsides of experiments in "living your best life," try Robyn Okrant's *Living Oprah: My One-Year Experiment to Walk the Walk of the Queen of Talk*. Find out more about "stunt memoirs" in the November chapter.

STUMBLING ON HAPPINESS

Daniel Gilbert

Ask children what they want to be when they grow up and you will likely get some funny answers like "Queen of the Pirates!" The child knows what interests her now, and she projects that she will still like the same things when she is older.

Celebrated psychologist Daniel Gilbert argues in his charming and funny book that all of us are in the same position as the child. We plan for the future using the imagination and experience we have today. Therefore, all our carefully laid plans may be as nonsensical as "I want to be a pirate" to our future selves. Gilbert claims that we make decisions for the people we are now rather than the people we will be. If you've ever reflected on a past decision and wondered what you could have been thinking, you will know exactly what he is talking about.

For all that it draws on psychology, philosophy, and neuroscience, *Stumbling on Happiness* is an accessible book. Gilbert takes us through the various things we mean when we use the word "happiness," as an emotion, a moral state, etc. He explains the ways the mind can be tricked into thinking that how it sees the world is the only way it can be seen. Using down-to-earth examples and a displaying a great sense of humor, Gilbert assures us that happiness is possible, but it probably won't be found through the mechanisms we usually employ to get it.

DISCUSSION/REFLECTION STRATEGIES

- Gilbert quotes Ernest Shackleton, the Antarctic explorer, who, when recounting a particularly dangerous part of his journey, referred to himself and his crew as "happy." Gilbert also quotes a man about to be executed for a crime that he did not commit as saying that this was "the happiest day of his life." Assuming we can trust both men to be telling the truth, what can we understand their definitions of happiness to be?

- How does happiness work for you? Is it a goal in your life or a by-product of achieving other goals? What are some things that are as important as or even more important than happiness?

EXTRA CREDIT

In the chapters to come, you will be reading books that are as much about happiness as they are about anything else. In February, the selections will emphasize that romantic love is a necessary ingredient in a happy life. In April, we will be looking at the role creativity plays in happiness and fulfillment. In the months and chapters ahead of you, keep asking yourself what the author of each book is championing as a necessary component of a happy life.

Mary Oliver

Felicity, Mary Oliver's most recent collection of poetry, is divided into two parts, "The Journey" and "Love," which might be Oliver's answers to the question, *What makes us happy?* (A third part, "Felicity," consists of just one poem.) Oliver writes about journeying as a metaphor for how we might live our best lives: journeys involve exploration and meandering. In Oliver's world, they don't necessarily involve destinations. Oliver is a keen observer of the natural world, mining nature for images and metaphors that illustrate what it means to be human, as well as finding wisdom and comfort in the way that plants and animals know their purpose and work in the world. For Oliver, wonder is a way of being in love with the world and of finding comfort, joy, and meaning in human existence. The love poems that make up the second half of this slender volume celebrate a passionate relationship that was unexpected, consuming, and life-affirming. A long relationship is, of course, a journey itself.

With people to love, questions to think about, work to do, and a world to observe, how can Oliver be anything but happy?

DISCUSSION/REFLECTION STRATEGIES

- It's difficult to read Mary Oliver's poetry without making personal connections and finding poems that seem to speak directly to our lives. Which poems resonate the most for you in this collection?
- Note that throughout the collection, Oliver uses the word "happiness" repeatedly, but "felicity" rarely occurs. In what ways do "happiness" and "felicity" differ?
- Like the poet Rumi (see below), Mary Oliver is a deeply spiritual poet, referencing the presence of God in all things. According to the section "The Journey," the increased sense of God's presence in her life more than compensates for the losses that come with old age. How does the poet express this? Does this make sense to you, and how does it make you feel?

Did You Know...?

The epigraphs to the three sections of *Felicity* all come from Rumi, a thirteenth-century Persian poet and Sufi mystic, whose poems focus on many of the questions that interest Oliver: What is the nature of beauty? What is faith, devotion? How can we best live and love? He may have died in 1273 in Turkey, but he remains one of the most popular poets in America. Coleman Banks's *Essential Rumi* is a good place to start. If you'd like to follow Oliver and read a poem by Rumi every day, you might like Coleman Banks's *A Year with Rumi: Daily Reading*.

EXTRA CREDIT

Oliver is the author of dozens of collections of poetry and essays. All are worth reading, but we particularly recommend *New and Selected Poems: Volume 1*, which won the National Book Award in 1992, and *Long Life*, a collection of essays (and a handful of poems) exploring life, writing, and nature.

Maira Kalman

What to do when confronted with inevitable tragedy? What to do when there is so much suffering and misery in the world? And, especially, what to do when we know we're going to die? "What is the point?" artist Maira Kalman asks again and again. It's the age-old conundrum human beings face: How is it possible to create a meaningful life when we are, in words she quotes from philosopher Bertrand Russell, "destined to extinction"?

The Principles of Uncertainty chronicles a year in Kalman's life as she experiences existential angst and examines the sources of happiness from many angles. Luckily, Kalman is equal to the task of finding meaning and purpose in the most mundane experiences. In fact, Kalman's answer to the question of how to find happiness when we're all going to die is rooted in the mundane. Go for a walk. Eat a piece of good chocolate. Admire a particularly fine mustache or a "superlative tassel." Kalman seeks "meaningful distraction" in the magnificent world around her, and her ability to find that delight is truly the source of her happiness. And the beautiful paintings Kalman creates in response to the world are another source of happiness for readers of this book.

DISCUSSION/REFLECTION STRATEGIES

- Kalman joins legions of writers, artists, and philosophers when she ponders questions of life's meaning and value. How do *you* find meaning and value? When you think of your own times of tragedy, suffering, or just plain boredom, how do you comfort yourself and return to life and happiness? Your group may want to do a "show and tell," sharing items (whether artifacts, poems, or prose passages) that consistently connect you to happiness.

Did You Know...?

A *flâneur* was someone who strolled around the city, observing the urban landscape and the ways people interact within that space. French poet Charles Baudelaire captured the experience in these words: "For the perfect *flâneur*, for the passionate spectator, it is an immense joy to set up house in the heart of the multitude, amid the ebb and flow of movement, in the midst of the fugitive and the infinite. To be away from home and yet to feel oneself everywhere at home; to see the world, to be at the center of the world, and yet to remain hidden from the world—impartial natures which the tongue can but clumsily define." Kalman's pleasure in city walks, subway rides, and people watching places her firmly in the tradition of the French *flâneur*.

EXTRA CREDIT

Maira Kalman's work explores the power and meaning of images and objects. If you'd like to explore image and creativity more deeply, check out cartoonist Lynda Barry's book, *What It Is*, an incredible illustrated memoir-workbook for writers that focuses on how objects and images trigger memory and creativity.

Laurie Colwin

This is a story of two couples: Guido and Holly, and Vincent and Misty. Guido and Vincent are third cousins. Guido sees Holly at a museum and decides he must know her. Vincent meets Misty at work, and though she's not the easiest person to get to know, he falls deeply in love. It's the late 1970s, they all live in Cambridge, Massachusetts and New York, and while each of the four is sane, intelligent, and holds good intentions, well… The course of true love never did run smooth.

If you are a fan of complicated plots and action sequences, then this is not the book for you. You will treasure this novel for its dialogue—it's very funny—and the exquisitely drawn portraits of people; not just the main characters but also the people who surround them like friends, relatives, and coworkers who are also all looking for happiness in their own ways.

DISCUSSION/REFLECTION STRATEGIES

- This novel is set in the late 1970s, not so long ago to be considered a historical work, but not contemporary either. Do any of the social mores take you by surprise? Is this how you thought (or remembered) the seventies to be?

- Some argue that Colwin's characters live lives of ease and privilege, making their dilemmas difficult to empathize with. They could be said to be suffering from the problems brought about by affluence. Is this a fair criticism of the work?

- Why is the book called *Happy All the Time*? Is this sarcasm? Or do the characters live actual happy lives? What is happiness as defined by this novel?

Did You Know...?

Commenters frequently call Laurie Colwin a modern-day Jane Austen. They make the comparison based on Colwin's penchant for witty dialogue, her focus on courtship rituals and relationships, and her finely drawn characters. Remember that Jane Austen referred to her own novels as worked on "a little bit (two inches wide) of ivory." She did not focus on grand, sweeping sagas but drew small pictures with large implications.

EXTRA CREDIT

If you are a fan of novels written in domestic settings and driven by dialogue and character sketches, then you will enjoy the work of Barbara Pym and Elizabeth Jane Howard.

Working on a deceptively small scale is Barbara Pym (1913–1980), an English writer whose many novels are all about the lives of women in postwar Britain. Pym was prolific, so you have a lot to choose from. Start with *Some Tame Gazelle*, *Excellent Women*, *Jane and Prudence*, *Less Than Angels*, and *A Glass of Blessings*.

There is an excellent biography of Pym, *A Lot to Ask: A Life of Barbara Pym*, by Hazel Holt.

Elizabeth Jane Howard (1923–2014), also English, wrote about domestic lives during the Second World War and after. She is best known for *The Cazalet Chronicle*, a five-novel family saga published between 1990 and 2013. Her autobiography, *Slipstream*, was published in 2002.

February

CLASSIC ROMANCE

- *Pride and Prejudice* by Jane Austen
- *Venetia* by Georgette Heyer
- *Tremaine's True Love* by Grace Burrowes
- *The Bollywood Bride* by Sonali Dev
- *Modern Romance* by Aziz Ansari and Eric Klinenberg

After all the introspection of last month, it's time to take a cue from St. Valentine and start looking at other people. Romance is our theme, and each selection celebrates romantic love in a different way. Get out your chocolates, sit in front of the fire, and dig in.

PRIDE AND PREJUDICE

Jane Austen

If you are a devotee of Jane Austen and her work, you already know how much you are going to enjoy reading or rereading *Pride and Prejudice*. If you have never read Austen before, we envy your first-time experience. For those who love Austen, the only sour note to her work is that it is finite.

Published anonymously in 1813, *Pride and Prejudice* is the story of the five Bennet sisters, ranging in age from fifteen to twenty-three. At the center of the plot are Mrs. Bennet's machinations to get her daughters married to eligible men. As Austen explores the complexities of family relationships, friendship, and love, she focuses on Elizabeth Bennet, who learns the personal meanings of the two title words: how her own pride has blinded her and fostered her prejudice.

From its beginnings in the early to mid-eighteenth century, the novel as a genre has focused on the pursuit of romantic love. *Pride and Prejudice* is no exception, but much of its beauty lies in its humor. What surprises first-time readers of Jane Austen is just how funny she is, with comedy arising not only from the situation and the story, but also from her language.

DISCUSSION/REFLECTION STRATEGIES

- Why is Elizabeth horrified by Charlotte's decision to marry Mr. Collins? Based on your understanding of Charlotte's position about marriage as well as Elizabeth's reasons for objecting, is Charlotte doing the right thing?

- Austen, who never married, was interested in what makes for a good partnership. Austen clearly wants us to believe that Elizabeth and Darcy, and also Jane and Bingley, will be happily married. She strongly suggests that people with good sense—like the Gardiners, for example—have good marriages.

Based on the character traits of these couples, what constitutes good sense for Austen, and what makes for a good marriage?

EXTRA CREDIT

Jane Austen was a young forty-two years old when she died, leaving only six completed novels and generations of bereft fans clamoring for more. Her work has inspired a myriad of tie-in and follow-up novels. If you cannot quite let go of the Bennets and Darcys, you might find some of the following retellings appealing.

- *Darcy and Fitzwilliam: A Tale of an Officer and a Gentleman* by Karen V. Wasylowski. An entertaining account of the relationship between the cousins.

- *Letters from Pemberley: The First Year* by Jane Dawkins. Dawkins tells the story of the Darcys' first year of marriage through letters written by Elizabeth to her sister Jane.

- *Death Comes to Pemberley* by P. D. James. Imagine the fictional world created by Austen infused with the mystery and intrigue of P. D. James and you have an amazing piece of fiction and a wonderful made-for-television miniseries as well.

- *The Lizzie Bennet Diaries* is the first YouTube series ever to win an Emmy. Lizzie's story is reimagined in a contemporary setting, with Lizzie vlogging about her life as a grad student while still living with her parents. Go to PemberleyDigital.com to find out more.

Have You Seen the Movie?

The last twenty years have seen a great number of film and made-for-television adaptations of Austen's novels, leading to one important question:

Who is the best Austen hero on-screen? Is it Colin Firth as Mr. Darcy? Rupert Penry-Jones as Captain Wentworth? Or Hugh Grant as Edward Ferrars? What about Alan Rickman as Colonel Brandon? Cue up some clips on YouTube, and we guarantee this will have your book group talking for some time.

VENETIA

Georgette Heyer

ℓ

Venetia Lanyon is a beautiful young woman who lives in Yorkshire with her younger brother. Her father's death and her elder brother's absence in the Napoleonic Wars mean that she manages the family's estate. Fortunately for her and the reader, Venetia is endowed with uncommon good sense, a direct manner, and a healthy wit. She's a romantic heroine, but she neither swoons nor grows pale. She is self-reliant and intelligent, and has only a moderate regard for the strictures of fashionable society. The combination of beauty, forthrightness, and wit has brought her two suitors: a worthy but boring neighborhood squire, and a romantic young man who fancies himself a spiritual successor to Lord Byron. Venetia does not find either of them appealing but thinks she should marry before her elder brother comes home with a bride. However, a chance encounter with the notorious Lord Damerel, making the rare visit to his Yorkshire estate, changes Venetia's life forever.

Heyer wrote twenty-four novels taking place during the Regency, and she was an expert on the period's manners, morals, and details of everyday life. Though her novels are practically textbooks, she instructs with a light touch, and it is a credit to her skill that Venetia and Damerel emerge as characters worth caring about and laughing with.

DISCUSSION/REFLECTION STRATEGIES

- Any work of fiction set in the past is likely, no matter how well researched, to bear traces of the time period in which it is *written* rather than the time period in which it is *set*. *Venetia* was written in 1958. Can you find anything in the text that sounds more like the concerns of twentieth-century women than those of the early nineteenth century? What about Venetia herself? To what extent do you think she is an accurate portrayal of what a woman could be like during this time period?

- What are we to do with the scene where Venetia and Lord Damerel meet? Is it safe to say that Damerel's behavior would not be acceptable in real life? How does this affect your ability to empathize with him and believe in the relationship between the two protagonists?

Did You Know...?

The Regency era is the period in British history from 1811 to 1820. When King George III was deemed unfit to rule, his son, the future George IV, ruled as Prince Regent in his stead.

Regency romances are a subgenre of romance novels and were invented by Georgette Heyer. In fact, she is credited with inventing the historical romance novel. Regency romances take place in the early nineteenth century and feature upper-class British characters. The characters are usually torn between their desires and their sense of propriety. Though traditionally regency romances did not have explicit sex scenes, times have changed, and so has the genre.

TREMAINE'S TRUE LOVE

Grace Burrowes

ℓ

Nita Haddonfield is one of the many siblings of the Earl of Bellefonte, who recently came into his title on the death of his father. Nita was her widowed father's favorite and managed his household. Now, with her sister-in-law in charge, Nita is free to follow her true passion: meeting the medical needs of the local villagers. She is knowledgeable and experienced in the sickroom. Her family worries for her (and their own) health as she deals, apparently fearlessly, with contagious diseases. It is their dearest wish that she marry and settle down to raising children and running her own home.

As if made to order, Tremaine St. Michael arrives as a guest of the Earl to discuss a business deal. St. Michael is good-looking, wealthy, and deeply impressed with Lady Nita. Nita and Tremaine are immediately attracted to one another. But is attraction enough for a lasting relationship? Can Nita and Tremaine learn to love one another as they really are?

DISCUSSION/REFLECTION STRATEGIES

- Both Nita and Tremaine have lost their parents. What do we know about Nita's parents, and how does that information illuminate her anxiety about forming a relationship with Tremaine? What about Nita's siblings? Are they all acting out a script written by their parents? Are they a "healthy" family, and what does that mean to you?

- Tremaine St. Michael is surprisingly candid about his resentment toward his parents. What does he resent them for? Does their manner of death have anything to do with the strictures Tremaine attempts to enforce upon Nita?

- What do you think are the key features of a romantic novel, like *Tremaine's True Love*, and how do these features differ from real life? What do you think makes fans of the genre so devoted to it?

Did You Know...?

Though *Tremaine's True Love* is fictional, the tension between Nita Haddonfield and the local physician, Dr. Horton, about methods of healing is based on historical fact. Medicine has a long tradition of leaving practical nursing and midwifery to women while denying them professional education and qualifications. If you're interested in finding out more, check out *Witches, Midwives, and Nurses: A History of Women Healers* by Barbara Ehrenreich and Deirdre English.

THE BOLLYWOOD BRIDE

Sonali Dev

Ria Parkar is a big star in Bollywood. Known as the "Ice Princess," she defies all paparazzi attempts to break through her cold exterior. But behind the facade of cool perfection is a passionate woman with a past of sorrow and trauma that she cannot bear to even think about. Ria knows that if she attempts to confront her past, all her carefully constructed fame is in danger of falling apart.

Yet, defying her own cautious code of conduct, she accepts an invitation to a beloved cousin's wedding in Chicago. It has been ten years since she was there, and she knows that the trip will bring her into contact with her former lover Vikram, whom she abandoned to start her film career.

What follows is an engrossing story of family gained and lost. Ria does meet Vikram, who has a new lover; old wounds are reopened, but old passion is renewed as well. Her aunts, uncles, and cousins remind Ria of what she lost when she left Chicago, but also throw into sharp relief the reasons she left in the first place. Is there a place in the world of warmth and love for Ria, or is she destined to be the Ice Princess forever?

DISCUSSION/REFLECTION STRATEGIES

- Weddings, with all their pomp and panic, ritual and romance, feature prominently in this novel. What are some wedding-related rituals you are familiar with, and how have they evolved over time? What do you think is the point of the rituals?

- Though romance novels are usually thought to be about two people in the throes of passion (and we can certainly see that in *The Bollywood Bride*), in the novels we look at this month we see a surprising influence of extended family on even the most self-absorbed couples. How does Ria draw strength from her family, even though she has been away for ten years? In your experience, is this how families work?

EXTRA CREDIT

It would be wonderful if this book came with illustrations, because all the characters' clothes sound so gorgeous! If you are not familiar with Indian saris, there are plenty of online resources to get you up to speed. Visit the website of London's Victoria and Albert Museum and search through their online collection. Better yet, if there is a sari store in your town, go have a browse.

- - - - - - - - -

 ## Have You Seen the Movie?

Hooray for Bollywood! "Bollywood" is the term for the Hindi-language film industry based in Mumbai. It is the most prolific film industry in the world. Bollywood films are usually musicals featuring elaborate song-and-dance numbers. The plots are frequently melodramas, the costumes are elaborate, and the stars are gorgeous. Bollywood films are great fun to watch. For starters, take a look at *Monsoon Wedding* (2001) and *Bride and Prejudice* (2004).

MODERN ROMANCE

Aziz Ansari and Eric Klinenberg

Modern Romance is a wonderful work of nonfiction on contemporary romantic practices. Authored by Aziz Ansari, whom you may know as an actor and stand-up comedian, this is a substantive analysis of the role technology plays in our love lives. Ansari teamed up with sociologist Eric Klinenberg, and together they designed a research project asking thousands of people from around the globe how they use social media and online dating sites for meeting potential romantic partners. Ansari and Klinenberg also talk to older people who met and married their partners before the dawn of the digital age, and study how people in non-Western cultures engage in modern romance.

Ansari's book covers such topics as whether it is better to contact a new interest via texting or a phone call. How does online dating work, and is there still a reluctance to admit to having done it? When does a lot of choice become too much choice? (If you've ever been overwhelmed by options in a supermarket and have left empty-handed, you will know what he's talking about.)

What interests Ansari most is not just how people got together fifty years ago and how they get together now, but how what people are looking for in a mate has changed. There was a time when, for most people, finding someone companionable was more than enough. These days, we insist on finding soul mates, and we have plenty of technological tools to help us in the quest. Whether our lives are easier and our quests successful due to technology is one of the main questions of the book.

DISCUSSION/REFLECTION STRATEGIES

- Whether reflecting on these issues on your own or discussing them in a group, *Modern Romance* is going to give you a lot to think about. How has the process of meeting potential partners changed in your lifetime?

- Ansari does a wonderful comparison between the time his father spent deciding which of the young women approved by his parents he would marry, and the much longer period of time Ansari spends deliberating about where to have brunch. You may have an arranged marriage or know someone who has one. How did it come about?

- Have your own ideas about what makes a good marriage changed for you over the course of your life? If your ideas have changed, then do you seek out people through different means than you did in the past?

EXTRA CREDIT

Look for an interview with Aziz Ansari about this book on npr.org. Videotaped appearances by both authors are available on YouTube.com.

March

FOCUS ON JUSTICE

- *March: Book One* by John Lewis, Andrew Aydin, and Nate Powell
- *Missoula: Rape and the Justice System in a College Town* by Jon Krakauer
- *Just Mercy: A Story of Justice and Redemption* by Bryan Stevenson
- *Citizen: An American Lyric* by Claudia Rankine
- *I am Malala: The Girl Who Stood Up for Education and Was Shot by the Taliban* by Malala Yousafzai and Christina Lamb

The topic for March is justice. Some of these books touch on concerns about policing, courts, and prisons. All of them touch on our fundamental need to be seen, heard, and acknowledged as full members of the society in which we live—and on the ways in which, for many of us, that need is not met.

John Lewis, Andrew Aydin, and Nate Powell

March is a graphic novel memoir written by Georgia Congressman John Lewis, an important figure in the Civil Rights Movement, and Andrew Aydin. Artist Nate Powell illustrates the book, the first of a projected trilogy. The narrative blends two timelines: there are present-day scenes set in Lewis's office in Washington, D.C., as he visits with some of his constituents; and there are lengthy flashbacks to Lewis's childhood on a farm in Alabama, his experiences growing up in a segregated community, and his early work in the Civil Rights Movement. Lewis has led an incredibly interesting and important life, and the graphic novel format proves to be a surprisingly effective way to tell his story.

Though he is aware of racial discrimination even as a small child, when Lewis starts school, he begins to experience the effects of segregation more sharply. He doesn't have the same opportunities as white children. In his adolescent years, he begins reading about Civil Rights activism in the local newspapers. The Montgomery Bus Boycott organized by Dr. Martin Luther King Jr. takes place just fifty miles from Lewis's hometown. He feels as though he is somehow involved too, and soon enough, he is taking an active role in protests, especially in lunch counter sit-ins. Book One ends with Lewis sitting at a lunch counter with other African Americans, hoping for a peaceful resolution to segregation. The fight for justice continues in *March: Book Two*.

DISCUSSION/REFLECTION STRATEGIES

- Laws officially ended segregation years ago, but subtle and not-so-subtle separations based on race and culture continue today. What examples are you aware of, either personally or through the news? What evidence of discrimination do you see in your community or workplace?

Did You Know...?

March was awarded a **Coretta Scott King Author Honor Award** in 2014. These awards honor African American authors and illustrators who write books for children and young adults that "promote understanding and appreciation of [African American] culture." Many Coretta Scott King Award recipients focus on the Civil Rights Movement, making the list of award winners an excellent resource for further study in the Civil Rights Movement.

EXTRA CREDIT

One source of inspiration for *March* is the sixteen-page comic *Martin Luther King and the Montgomery Story* published in 1957. It was produced to tell the story of the Montgomery Bus Boycott and was distributed to community groups, churches, and schools. The comic also sets forth the principles of nonviolence resistance, traces the roots of nonviolent resistance to the work of Mahatma Gandhi, and serves as an instruction manual on activism. Though ignored by the mainstream press, the comic was influential in the Civil Rights Movement and in similar movements around the world. The comic is in print again—having been reissued by Top Shelf Comics in 2013.

MISSOULA: RAPE AND THE JUSTICE SYSTEM IN A COLLEGE TOWN

Jon Krakauer

Over a three-year period in Missoula, Montana, at least eighty rapes were reported, leading some newspapers and websites to dub the town of roughly 70,000 people the "rape capital" of America. Unfortunately, Missoula is far from being America's rape capital. In fact, the number of reported rapes in Missoula matches the national average for a town of its size over the same time period. And, as Krakauer reminds the reader, national rape statistics are based on reported cases, which are believed to be only a small percentage of the actual total number of sexual assaults that occur every year. Krakauer takes us deep into the stories of five of these eighty-plus victims in Missoula. We get to know the victims, as well as other key people involved, including their family members and friends and the police officers and attorneys investigating and prosecuting these cases, as the author paints a picture of a crime that is all too prevalent in America.

Because this is a book of investigative journalism, Krakauer focuses on telling the story accurately and objectively. Still, outrage simmers on nearly every page. Krakauer's book is a difficult, at times maddening read, but it should also be required reading for all Americans. Ultimately, Krakauer writes a damning expose of a culture in which rape "occurs with appalling frequency" and is rarely prosecuted effectively, a culture we must all take responsibility for changing.

DISCUSSION/REFLECTION STRATEGIES

- Are you and your book group surprised by the stories and statistics Krakauer presents in this book? What other emotions do you experience as you read these accounts?

- Krakauer suggests changes in police and legal procedures that will make it easier and more effective to prosecute rapes as well as support victims. What do you think could be done to prevent so many sexual assaults from happening in the first place?

Did You Know...?

Rape culture is the term used to describe a phenomenon whereby sexual violence is considered the norm and the onus is on potential victims to avoid being assaulted. If you are interested in finding out more about rape culture, visit EverydaySexism.com, a crowd-sourced site where people contribute stories of harassment and abuse encountered every day.

EXTRA CREDIT

For an impassioned and provocative analysis of American rape culture, read Kate Harding's *Asking for It: The Alarming Rise of Rape Culture—And What We Can Do about It*. Also take a look at *We Should All Be Feminists* by Chimamanda Ngozi Adichie.

JUST MERCY: A STORY OF JUSTICE AND REDEMPTION

Bryan Stevenson

Attorney Bryan Stevenson discovered his life's work when he was just twenty-three years old and interning for a law firm in Georgia. His task was simple: deliver a message to a man on death row. Little did he know that inter-action would give a new focus to his life. Ever since, Stevenson has advocated tirelessly for compassion, mercy, and justice for those who have been wrongly accused and condemned by our flawed judicial system. Stevenson takes the cases of those who have been most marginalized and disenfranchised: children, the poor, racial minorities, and the mentally ill.

Although Stevenson weaves in examples from cases throughout his career to support his claim that the judicial system is "defined by error," the main story he shares is that of Walter McMillan, a black man who was falsely accused of murdering a white woman in Alabama and spent six years on death row. There was virtually no evidence to link McMillan to the crime. In fact, he was at a barbecue with over one hundred people at the time of the murder, but even with over a hundred eyewitnesses, he couldn't get a fair trial. The evidence in many of Stevenson's cases is just as obvious, and the results of these trials condemning the clearly innocent or the mentally ill are just as outrageous.

The work Stevenson and his colleagues do is nothing short of heroic. And while many of us would see this as righteous work, others find him and his legal practice so threatening that they make death threats. Stevenson and his colleagues must routinely clear out of their offices for the afternoon while the bomb squad searches the building for bombs. *Just Mercy* is a damning exposé of a judicial system that is at best overworked and inefficient, and at worst racist and corrupt.

DISCUSSION/REFLECTION STRATEGIES

- Stevenson argues that the death penalty debate shouldn't focus on whether a person deserves to die for their crimes; rather, we need to ask ourselves, Do we deserve to kill? How does Stevenson try to answer that question in *Just Mercy*? How were your own thoughts or beliefs challenged by reading these accounts of injustice and suffering?

Did You Know...?

The Equal Justice Initiative is Bryan Stevenson's organization, which advocates for prison reform, especially abolition of the death penalty; reform to laws that allow children to be tried and sentenced as adults and sent to adult prisons; and relief for the mentally ill who are currently housed in prison. On its website, eji.org, you can access interviews with Bryan Stevenson, articles about EJI's work, and research about poverty and racial inequality in the judicial system, as well as learn more about how to get involved and work for change.

EXTRA CREDIT

Bryan Stevenson's TED Talk, "We Need to Talk about an Injustice," has been viewed over 2.5 million times. In this talk, he blends personal history and social history to explain why the work he does is so important and how it affects all Americans. The talk can be accessed at Ted.com.

— — — — — — — —

CITIZEN: AN AMERICAN LYRIC

Claudia Rankine

Claudia Rankine's collection of prose poems, *Citizen*, reports and examines the racial aggressions Black Americans experience as part of their daily lives, often in the most mundane circumstances—in line at the drugstore, sitting on an airplane waiting for takeoff—and often from people whose racist words come as a shock—colleagues at work, a longtime friend. Rankine describes the psychic effects of such constant small attacks, the hypervigilance such experiences inevitably prompt, and the profound discomfort felt in public and private spaces when emotional, physical, and mental safety cannot be guaranteed.

Citizen is a hybrid work, combining essay, poem, and image. Part meditation, part analysis, the short pieces in this collection provoke and challenge the reader to consider what it means to be a citizen. How can a person enjoy the full rights and privileges of citizenship when, at any moment, those rights and privileges can be revoked?

DISCUSSION/REFLECTION STRATEGIES

- Many readers have questioned what makes this hybrid, innovative book a work of poetry. Why do you think Rankine chooses to write prose poems in straightforward, everyday speech? What connections can you make between Rankine's form and her subject matter? How does the inclusion of photos enrich your understanding of the poems?

- The book includes an extended essay on tennis superstars Venus and Serena Williams. It also addresses the church shooting at the Emanuel African Methodist Episcopal Church in Charleston in 2015. How does the variety in the subject matter affect your reading? How does Rankine's presentation speak to you?

Did You Know...?

Citizen is subtitled "An American Lyric." **Lyric poetry** was developed in Ancient Greece as a form of spoken poetry meant to be accompanied by a musical instrument. A lyric poem typically focuses on a personal emotional experience.

EXTRA CREDIT

Ta-Nehisi Coates's *Between the World and Me* is a searingly written, provocative investigation of America's race problem, a must-read after Rankine's *Citizen*. Another way to extend your understanding of Rankine's poems is to watch her perform these pieces. There are many readings available to view on YouTube.

I AM MALALA: THE GIRL WHO STOOD UP FOR EDUCATION AND WAS SHOT BY THE TALIBAN

Malala Yousafzai
with Christina Lamb

I Am Malala is the inspiring true story of Malala Yousafzai, a girl from Pakistan who came to international attention when, at the age of fifteen, she was shot by the Taliban outside her school. Her outspoken beliefs and her own insistence on attending school made her a target for the Taliban, who destroyed hundreds of schools in Pakistan and threatened and terrorized those who believed women had the right to an education. However, Malala is probably targeted as much for her father's outspoken beliefs and actions as for her own, and he emerges as the first great hero of this story. He created a school where both boys and girls could be educated, offering tuition-free seats in his school for poor children, and he still speaks out tirelessly for the right of all Pakistani children to receive an education. He knows the likely consequences for his actions under the Taliban, who ruthlessly target those who do not share their extremist beliefs, but he is unwilling to live in fear. Even more heroically, he will not allow his daughter to be afraid and encourages her to speak out for her beliefs as well.

I Am Malala is a deeply personal book that also tells the story of a culture and a way of life that is threatened under the Taliban reign of terror. Malala's love for her home, people, and culture is a strong theme throughout, and the reader can't help but feel her pain at being exiled from the place she loves. Incredibly, she turns tragedy into opportunity, arguing that she does not regret anything that has happened to her since she has discovered her life's mission: to speak out against injustice.

DISCUSSION/REFLECTION STRATEGIES

- What surprises you most about Malala's story?
- We may not always be able to affect the world political stage, but what could be done in your own community and city to ensure safety and

opportunity for all girls and women? Are there other international situations that Malala's story brings to mind?

- How do the schools in your community ensure that education is available to everyone?

Did You Know...?

In 2014, Malala was awarded the **Nobel Peace Prize** jointly with Kailash Satyarthi, an Indian activist for children's rights. Look for Malala's impassioned acceptance speech on YouTube.

EXTRA CREDIT

The Malala Fund is an organization created by Malala Yousafzai and her family to support education rights activism for girls and women. At their website, Malala .org, you can read stories about different projects funded by the Malala Fund and contribute yourself through volunteering or donating money.

CREATIVE SPIRIT

- *Everything Leads to You* by Nina LaCour
- *Page by Paige* by Laura Lee Gulledge
- *The Creative Habit: Learn It and Use It for Life* by Twyla Tharp
- *The Rise: Creativity, the Gift of Failure, and the Search for Mastery* by Sarah Lewis
- *Crazy Brave* by Joy Harjo

Spring is traditionally a time when we think about new life—trees coming into bud, seeds sending shoots peeking through the soil. And we also think about the care and nurturing these vulnerable beginnings require if they are to achieve a hardy maturity. This month's tales feature a variety of people whose desire to live creative, vibrant lives risks being cut down before they even get properly started. Read on to see if they make it…

EVERYTHING LEADS TO YOU

Nina LaCour

Nina LaCour's hopeful young-adult novel—but perfect for any age—begins in sorrow: Emi's girlfriend has just broken up with her for what seems like the millionth time, and she's not sure how she's going to cope. She has wonderful parents, a terrific best friend, and a dream job designing sets for a film studio in Hollywood. She even has a special treat: the use of her brother's apartment for the summer while he's off scouting sets in London. Still, she can't stop pining for her ex-girlfriend. Emi can't help but see life as a movie, and she's handed a great plot with terrific characters when she and her best friend Charlotte discover a letter from a dead movie star to an unknown woman. They manage to deliver the letter, though not to the person it's addressed to, and in the process of solving the noirish mystery, Emi's own life is immeasurably enriched and broadened.

Emi's job is one of the most interesting parts of this novel, and LaCour writes beautifully about the false starts, dead ends, and just plain serendipity of any creative endeavor. Certainly Emi's job invites her to express her creativity and even to philosophize about the importance of objects: "The art department creates the world. When you walk into someone's house and you see all of their things—the neatness or the clutter, the objects they have on display—that's when you really know someone." But Emi is also creating herself through her work and through her relationships. Her work as a set designer can be read as a metaphor for the work of her life—figuring out what matters to her, getting to know herself, expressing herself and her needs and desires.

DISCUSSION/REFLECTION STRATEGIES

- In the acknowledgments, Nina LaCour shares the story of how this novel came to be. When visiting a high school in Minnesota, she met with the Gay-Straight Alliance: "They taught me how important it is to share stories about love and hope." Why do you think it was important to the students in this GSA group to read stories of "love and hope"?

- As the quote above says, every object tells a story and, more importantly, tells us something about the person who owns it. To what extent do you think this is true?

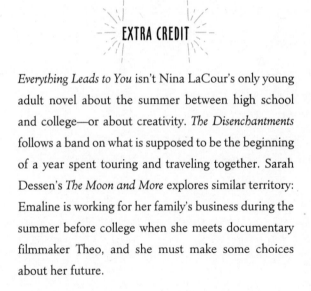

EXTRA CREDIT

Everything Leads to You isn't Nina LaCour's only young adult novel about the summer between high school and college—or about creativity. *The Disenchantments* follows a band on what is supposed to be the beginning of a year spent touring and traveling together. Sarah Dessen's *The Moon and More* explores similar territory: Emaline is working for her family's business during the summer before college when she meets documentary filmmaker Theo, and she must make some choices about her future.

PAGE BY PAIGE

Laura Lee Gulledge

Budding artist Paige has just moved to New York City with her writer parents, leaving behind her beloved friends and life in Virginia. Things are strained at home, and Paige initially feels overwhelmed by the city—all its sights, sounds, smells, people—and she is missing Virginia. It's the middle of the school year, and she doesn't know how she's going to make new friends or find a way to fit in. But she does have a source of consolation and comfort: her new sketchbook and the rules her artist grandmother shared with her about creating art.

Like many young artists, Paige is full of insecurities and self-doubt. In this beautiful graphic novel, Gulledge's illustrations brilliantly convey the reality of Paige's physical world and the musings of her imagination, and her drawings show an artist who is growing in confidence and mastery. Paige's commitment to following her grandmother's artistic rules helps, and so does befriending a group of creative types at school. Her new friends are curious about Paige's art and supportive once she finds the confidence to share her work.

DISCUSSION/REFLECTION STRATEGIES

- Gulledge draws elaborate metaphors to represent Paige's feelings and understanding of the world. Which illustrations particularly stand out for you, and why?

- In this story, Paige has to resolve her own particular adolescent angst. What connections do you make between Paige's worries and concerns and your own memories of adolescence?

- This is a coming-of-age graphic novel in which the heroine learns to feel more at home in her world and develops confidence in her abilities. Do you feel that this is a realistic portrayal of a sensitive teen's life? Do you remember feeling awkward as a teen, and what advice would you give to Paige?

Did You Know...?

Many artists use sketchbook challenges like Paige's to inspire their work and help them develop regular creative routines. You don't need a special book to design a daily creativity challenge, but it couldn't hurt. Keri Smith's *Wreck This Journal* may be the most famous example of a creative journal with prompts that you can complete by sketching, writing, or creating. Check out Austin Kleon's *Steal Like an Artist Journal* for more ideas.

EXTRA CREDIT

Want to learn more about how comics work as a visual language? Scott McCloud's TED Talk, "The Visual Magic of Comics," explores how we process visual imagery and make sense of comics. McCloud is also the author of *Understanding Comics: The Invisible Art*, a study—in comics form!—of how comics and cartoons work.

THE CREATIVE HABIT: LEARN IT AND USE IT FOR LIFE

Twyla Tharp

The Creative Habit is a practical and inspirational guide to the conditions, habits, routines, and practices necessary for productive creative work, written by the prolific dancer and choreographer, Twyla Tharp. Tharp shares insights gleaned from her own long working life as well as examples from creative lives ranging from composers like Mozart to writers like Raymond Chandler, from golf champions like Arnold Palmer to "advertising wizards" like Phil Dusenberry. As Tharp confesses in the first chapter, she comes from the "hard work" school of creativity. She doesn't believe in divine inspiration or genius: she believes in hard work, plain and simple.

In this book, Tharp shares the practices she has developed over the years to ensure that she can be creatively productive. Different chapters focus on specific rituals and exercises Tharp uses to get her mind into a creative state and discover material for new dance productions. She shares techniques that help her weather rough patches in a project. She even reflects on the many important lessons she has learned from failure. Each chapter ends with a set of exercises that readers can do to develop their creative thinking and discover ideas for new projects.

DISCUSSION/REFLECTION STRATEGIES

- Tharp insists on the importance of having some concrete method for saving ideas. She tells of returning to a moment of past inspiration from which she creates a major performance, but she is only able to recall the inspiration because she has a box of clues and artifacts. What method do you use to hold on to your creative ideas until you are ready to act, and can you share a success story? Do you believe a strong work ethic is intrinsic or the result of habit?

- Think about your own creative endeavors—keeping in mind that we can be creative in any field. Do they start with ideas, or do ideas come through application?

Did You Know...?

Twyla Tharp is a pioneer in the rise of the **crossover ballet**, the fusion of classical ballet with popular music. Her first, produced in 1973, was *Deuce Coupe,* based on the work of the Beach Boys. Critics think her best crossover ballet is the 1976 *Push Comes to Shove*, starring Mikhail Baryshnikov. Videos of both are available on YouTube.

EXTRA CREDIT

Julia Cameron's *Artist's Way* is a twelve-week program designed to develop your creativity, free you from blocks, and give you more insight into yourself as a creative person. Many artists and writers swear by Cameron's Morning Pages, as well as by other exercises in this book.

THE RISE: CREATIVITY, THE GIFT OF FAILURE, AND THE SEARCH FOR MASTERY

Sarah Lewis

In *The Rise*, art curator, critic, and scholar Sarah Lewis examines the role of failure in creativity. Of course, she is particularly interested in the work of artists and writers, but she also draws many analogies from business, science, and even sports. In fact, she finds some of her guiding metaphors for this project in her observations of the women's archery team at Columbia University in New York City. This wide-ranging book argues that failure is an essential part of the creative process and the quest for mastery.

In fact, those whom we consider to be masters of their art or craft are rarely satisfied with the products of their labor. This is one of many paradoxes Lewis uncovers in her research into the history of innovative ideas and art.

Lewis is most interested in the psychological states and perspectives that make some people more receptive to creativity, more able to withstand failure, and more committed to their craft. This book is full of anecdotes and examples drawn from a broad spectrum of innovators and masters in different fields. You won't find specific creative strategies or suggestions in this book, but you will find thoughtful meditations on the value of silence and stillness, the power of walking, and the necessity of taking risks.

DISCUSSION/REFLECTION STRATEGIES

- Most of us would admit that failure and fear of failure have affected our own willingness to take creative risks. How is failure useful—even essential—to the creative process? In spite of this fear, how have you stretched yourself creatively, and what have you chosen not to attempt because of the possibility of failure?

EXTRA CREDIT

Elizabeth Gilbert's TED Talk, "Your Elusive Creative Genius," examines how writers and artists can approach failure and the fear of failure as well as success and its pressures. Like Lewis, she suggests that changing our perspective and understanding the psychology of creativity can make us more productive and well-adjusted artists. Gilbert's nonfiction book, *Big Magic: Creative Living Beyond Fear*, offers anecdotes, advice, and encouragement to creative types who struggle to get the work done.

Sarah Lewis herself gives a TED Talk called "Embrace the Near Win," which can be found on Ted.com.

Joy Harjo

Joy Harjo is a poet, playwright, visual artist, and musician. Her memoir is challenging, lyrical, and compelling reading. The author tells us about her grandparents, who they are and how they lived. She describes her parents' tempestuous relationship and divorce. Her description of her stepfather's tyranny is harrowing. Her escape through art and the company of fellow artists is joyful to behold. Yet information about her life is only part of the story. Read it to find out how Harjo opens herself to a wider vision of reality even while suffering the privations of poverty. Though bad things happen, she is never victimized; she is a poet, a conduit between worlds, living, breathing, and seeing things that the rest of us can only dream of.

While *Crazy Brave* is not a "how-to" book on creativity, it is a primer in allowing creativity into one's life, however dire one's circumstances may be.

DISCUSSION/REFLECTION STRATEGIES

- Does approaching geography from the vantage point of the spiritual open up any new vistas for you? Think about the way you approach East, North, West, and South. Do you prefer sunrise or sunsets? If you were to start walking without giving any conscious thought to your destination, would you turn right or left or some other way? Do you have a favorite direction? Keep in mind that you don't have to justify these leanings. In fact, don't even try. Do you know the cardinal points in relation to where you are right now without checking a compass?

- Harjo reports having premonitions, knowing that a particular course of action will lead to good or bad consequences (for example, when she attends the Institute of American Indian Arts instead of running off to San Francisco). How do you listen to the nonrational in your own life?

EXTRA CREDIT

Crazy Brave is filled with the author's poetry. Whether you are discussing this book in a group or reflecting on it yourself—stand up and read the poetry aloud. This is a book that is demanding to be read aloud! Why do the poems and stories appear in the memoir where they do? They do not always seem to be immediately relevant, but speaking the stories aloud will slowly reveal that their placement is no accident.

FAMILIES IN FICTION

- *A Home at the End of the World* by Michael Cunningham
- *The Star Side of Bird Hill* by Naomi A. Jackson
- *Under the Udala Trees* by Chinelo Okparanta
- *Please Look After Mom* by Kyung-Sook Shin
- *After the Parade* by Lori Ostlund

Our families are often the people we are closest to, the people we think we know best. But members of even the most tightly knit families can be bewildering and opaque to one another. In this month's selections we include books that make vivid that intense cocktail of love and longing, distance and disappointment, intimacy and mystery that makes up family life.

A HOME AT THE END OF THE WORLD

Michael Cunningham

A Home at the End of the World is about families of origin, which we don't get to choose, and the families we construct by choice. Jonathan and Bobby meet on the first day of middle school. Both come from families experiencing loss and estrangement. Both are drawn to one another, though neither would be able to say why. Years later, Jonathan meets Clare, and they form a tight bond, "half-lovers," and with the addition of Bobby, the three are determined to create a family from scratch—one that will enable the three of them—and hopefully a baby—to thrive.

But life, as Michael Cunningham shows us in this exquisitely moving novel, has its own plans. We follow the lives of Bobby, Jonathan, and Clare as they navigate New York City and the 1980s. We share their hopes and dreams as they strive to create a new kind of family.

DISCUSSION/REFLECTION STRATEGIES

- This novel opens with a poem by Wallace Stevens, "The Poem That Took the Place of a Mountain." Reread the poem after you have finished the novel, think about why Cunningham chose that poem to start the book, and look for the ways that the poem mirrors the novel.

- Pop culture references abound in the novel. What do the songs that people mention, the musicals they prefer, and the T-shirts they wear tell us about who they are? How do you express yourself through your popular culture choices?

- To what extent are the main characters successful in realizing their dreams? How happy are they at the end?

Have You Seen the Movie?

A Home at the End of the World was made into a film in 2004 starring Colin Farrell, Dallas Roberts, and Robin Wright Penn. Watch the film and compare it to the novel. Michael Cunningham also wrote *The Hours*, a critically acclaimed novel that also became a successful film in 2002, garnering an Oscar for Nicole Kidman.

Examining the choices directors make is a rich vein to mine for reflection or conversation. Why do situations or characters from novels get changed in films? What drives the change? What are your favorite adaptations of novels for film?

THE STAR SIDE OF BIRD HILL

Naomi Jackson

Sisters Dionne and Phaedra Rose live in New York with their mother. One summer, she sends them to her mother, Hyacinth, in Barbados so she can work on getting her life in order. Sixteen-year-old Dionne thinks she must have done something terrible to be punished with an entire summer living with her grandmother in a place where nothing ever happens. But ten-year-old Phaedra loves her grandmother (though she is a little bit frightened of her) and loves Barbados, which, though she was born in New York, feels immediately like home. Over the summer, Barbados works its magic on the sisters. They become closer to their grandmother. Their mother's letters become less frequent. One day their father shows up with his new girlfriend and wants to take the girls to Miami. Can they trust him? Where is their true home?

Naomi Jackson's debut novel is touching, warm, and often very funny. Grandmother Hyacinth is a rock of stability and moral rectitude, but even she feels at sea sometimes with her strong-willed granddaughters. The responsibility of caring for them makes her reflect on their mother, her own daughter, and how mothers and daughters support and yet test one another all the time.

DISCUSSION/REFLECTION STRATEGIES

- Hyacinth is the strongest character in the book, but she's not infallible. How does Hyacinth's role in the community affect how people treat the family? How important is she to Bird Hill?

- The three generations of women in the family have strong ties with the community and one another. How do these relationships change over the course of the novel?

- Consider the story Hyacinth tells Dionne about her great-great-grandmother, who was a slave. What are the challenges facing Dionne that do not face Phaedra? What does she have to learn?

Did You Know...?

The festival in the novel called *Crop Over* has its roots in the late seventeenth century. It is the traditional harvest festival of Barbados, originally celebrating the sugarcane harvest, and lasts several weeks. *Crop Over* is similar to the Trinidad Carnival, and it consists of parades, music, and dance, culminating in Kadooment Day, with calypso bands and parades of dancers and musicians. Kadooment Day is a national holiday in Barbados.

In *The Star Side of Bird Hill*, Hyacinth makes some references to being an "obeah" woman. **Obeah** is a West Indian term for folk magic, sorcery, religious and healing practices that date back to the religious traditions of West African slaves, particularly those of Igbo origin. Obeah is associated with healing but also malicious magic. Notice that in the novel, Hyacinth indignantly rejects any suggestion she practices "bad magic."

Chinelo Okparanta

ℯ

Under the Udala Trees is the debut novel by award-winning short story writer Chinelo Okparanta. It tells the story of Ijeoma, a young girl living with her parents in an upper-middle-class household during the war between Nigeria and Biafra. The war tears the family apart, and Ijeoma is sent to live with a friend of her father as a servant. There she meets Amina, another young woman, and they fall in love. Not only are they two women in love, but they are also divided by ethnicity and religion: Ijeoma is Igbo and Christian, Amina is Hausa and Muslim.

What follows is Ijeoma's struggle for acceptance and the freedom to live her life as she sees fit. Her mother is convinced she is possessed by a demon. The society in which she lives is not any more open to gay and lesbian relationships than her mother is. Ijeoma submits to traditional expectations, and she struggles to maintain an authentic sense of self.

This is not a novel that is just about "star-crossed lovers": it is also a novel about war, starvation, ethnic hatred, and fundamentalism. Despite the discord, Okparanta describes a childhood village of vivid beauty. The reader can see the colors, hear the sounds, and smell the scents of this near-Eden. This is a multifaceted novel that will stay with the reader for a long time.

DISCUSSION/REFLECTION STRATEGIES

- An allegory is, as Ijeoma notes in the book, a symbolic representation of a political or moral deeper meaning. Take, for example, the fable of the boy who cried wolf. It would be a serious misreading of that story to assume it is about, and *only* about, the finer points of being a child shepherd. It is a story instructing its hearers on the dangers of lying. Are the founding texts of Christianity, Judaism, and Islam to be read allegorically or literally? We don't expect you to answer this definitively in your book group or your journal, but it is a central question of our age and one that needs periodic revisiting.

Did You Know...?

Readers of a certain age will remember shocking photographs of starving Biafran children on magazines and television in the late 1960s. The defeat of Biafra by Nigeria was the result of a bloody civil war with long-lasting consequences— many of which are chronicled in Okparanta's novel. An informative BBC documentary on the Nigeria-Biafra War is available on YouTube. Other books addressing the war are Chimamanda Ngozi Adichie's *Half of a Yellow Sun* and Chinua Achebe's memoir *There Was a Country*.

PLEASE LOOK AFTER MOM

Kyung-Sook Shin

In this deeply moving novel from South Korea's highly regarded Kyung-Sook Shin, sixty-nine-year-old So-Nyo becomes separated from her husband at a Seoul train station and goes missing. Her grown children organize a search, buying ads in newspapers and handing out leaflets wherever they go. As weeks go by, the various people in So-Nyo's life reflect on their relationship to her. The children and husband she left behind are forced to confront what they knew and did not know of this central figure in their lives. Their own lives are transformed by their grief and guilt.

What emerges is a portrait in painstaking detail of the daily life of a woman who was wife, mother, neighbor, friend, and at the same time a mystery just beyond everyone's reach.

DISCUSSION/REFLECTION STRATEGIES

- A subtitle to this novel could be "The Changing Role of Motherhood." Who are the various mothers in the book, and what are their defining characteristics? Do all the memories of So-Nyo link up to a coherent, imaginable being, or are memory and time creating different So-Nyos for different characters?

- Certainly one of the most striking features of the novel is its account of rural South Korean life just after the Korean War. The family is growing up during a period of tremendous growth for South Korea. How do the novel and the family's changing fortunes reflect the transformation of South Korea during the past fifty years?

Did You Know...?

A **pietà** is a representation in Christian art of Mary, the mother of Jesus, holding his dead body in her arms. The most famous pietà is the one by Michelangelo in St. Peter's Basilica at the Vatican, completed in 1500. You might want to reread the last pages of the book with a picture of Michelangelo's pietà in front of you.

You may wish to consider the different types of narrators when reading *Please Look After Mom*. A **first-person narrator** is a character telling the story; she is a **naïve narrator** if she does not understand the entire story or an **unreliable narrator** if we suspect that the narration is not truthful. An **omniscient narrator** knows everything that is happening. An omniscient narrator who interjects personal opinion or explanations is called an **intrusive narrator**.

AFTER THE PARADE

Lori Ostlund

Aaron and Walter are a couple with a long relationship. Walter, who is older, "saved" Aaron when the younger man was an emotionally isolated gay eighteen-year-old in Minnesota. The novel opens with Aaron deciding to leave Walter. He believes that, having lived with abusive parents, uncomprehending neighbors, and his longtime lover, he needs the opportunity to live on his own and create a life of his own making. Aaron moves to San Francisco, takes an apartment behind a garage, and teaches English to immigrants in a poor, disorganized school.

The process of building a new life and creating a new family is difficult for Aaron. His lifelong feeling of being an outsider impacts his ability to cultivate relationships. His new way of life forces him to confront the abuse he suffered as a child, and the book is largely told in flashbacks. Ostlund tells the story of Aaron's father's physical abuse and his mother's emotional neglect in a direct, vivid manner. The book is emotionally difficult to read at times, but this story of a man coming to terms with his past and looking forward to his future is worth the effort.

DISCUSSION/REFLECTION STRATEGIES

- Think about Walter and Aaron's relationship. In what ways is it believable, and how convincing is their breakup?

- How does San Francisco meet Aaron's expectations? By the end of the novel, how far has Aaron gone in getting what he has dreamed of?

- In your experience, how useful is it to move to a new location to find a new way of life? To what extent do you think that people can reinvent themselves?

EXTRA CREDIT

In an interview with the author—which can be found on her website, LoriOstlund.com—she speaks of her time in Asia and says that she loved being an outsider there. She thinks that feeling of not-belonging is important to her as a writer.

Have you ever had the experience of being an outsider—whether living in another country or even another part of your own country—and how did you find it of value? Aaron is an outsider most of his life, and his experience is not a pleasant one, but is his experience valuable to him? Does his outsider status help him to grow?

FAMILIES IN NONFICTION

- *Becoming Nicole: The Transformation of an American Family* by Amy Ellis Nutt
- *Selfish, Shallow, and Self-Absorbed: Sixteen Writers on the Decision Not to Have Kids* edited by Meghan Daum
- *Can't We Talk about Something More Pleasant?* by Roz Chast
- *Pregnant Butch: Nine Long Months Spent in Drag* by A. K. Summers
- *The Beautiful Struggle: A Father, Two Sons, and an Unlikely Road to Manhood* by Ta-Nehisi Coates

We often think of family as a hand of cards we're dealt, as a fact that shapes our destiny rather than something we choose for ourselves. But for the families in this month's selections, it's not so simple—each of them has some work to do, and some choices to make, before they can truly become a family.

Amy Ellis Nutt

Becoming Nicole is the story of a family's transformation as they struggle to understand, accept, and ultimately advocate for their transgender child. Nicole Maines knew from a very young age that she was not a boy: before she was even three, she told her father that she hated her penis. At first, her parents simply thought she was a little different and would eventually grow out of it. But it soon became clear that Nicole knew exactly who she was—a girl. The problem, it turns out, wasn't with Nicole at all; rather, it was with those who struggled to accept who she was, starting with her own father. Wayne Maines's journey is especially poignant and brave, as he faces the most challenges to his personal belief system and values in the person of the daughter he thought was a son.

Amy Ellis Nutt weaves a biography of Nicole and her family with a journalistic account of a discrimination lawsuit, scientific research into the biology of gender, and psychological research into the formation of gender identity. This fascinating and important book raises so many questions about what it means to know, understand, and accept ourselves, as well as what it means to know, understand, and accept others, especially those we love most.

DISCUSSION/REFLECTION STRATEGIES

- How do you relate to the family, friends, and neighbors of the family? To what extent are people's responses understandable to you?

- State lawmakers are wrestling with questions on how transgender youth can be treated respectfully and fairly with regard to school bathrooms, sports teams, and locker rooms, while also addressing the concerns and rights of non-transgendered youth. Think about your own community; review any legislation on the subject of transgender rights that your state is currently considering.

- After reading Nutt's comprehensive presentation of transgender issues, how have your own ideas changed or evolved?

EXTRA CREDIT

There is an interview with Wayne and Kelly Maines on the NPR program *Fresh Air*. See npr.org.

Jennifer Finney Boylan's *She's Not There: A Life in Two Genders* shares Boylan's personal story of transforming from James to Jennifer in her forties. Boylan's parenting memoir, *Stuck in the Middle with You: A Memoir of Parenting in Three Genders*, shares her story of parenting for the first few years of her sons' lives as their father, where her parenting role seemed fairly well defined, then transitioning to a woman and a new parenting role. For a more in-depth look at the particular struggles of transgender teens, read Susan Kuklin's remarkable collection of interviews and photographs, *Beyond Magenta: Transgender Teens Speak Out*.

SELFISH, SHALLOW, AND SELF-ABSORBED: SIXTEEN WRITERS ON THE DECISION NOT TO HAVE KIDS

Edited by Meghan Daum

The title of this collection of essays is meant to provoke a reaction. *Selfish*, *shallow*, and *self-absorbed* are adjectives the childless-by-choice have heard others use to describe their decision; however, the essays in this collection are anything but. Daum notes in her introduction that people choose not to have children for a myriad of reasons—physical, emotional, political, professional, spiritual. What's common among these essays, however, is that being childless by choice requires soul-searching and intentionality. Many of the contributors always thought they would have children but ultimately found compelling reasons not to. These essayists must develop narratives for themselves and their lives and find fulfillment through extended family, work, friendship, and other interests.

Work is a constant theme in this collection, as many contributors find parenthood and childcare particularly incompatible with the demands of their work. Families of origin are also a constant theme. Just as mothers and fathers must confront their own upbringings in order to parent their children effectively and intentionally, childless adults also find themselves coming to terms with the feelings, experiences, and examples of their childhoods as they make the decision not to have children. While a collection of essays about the decision to remain childless might seem to appeal most naturally to childless readers, in truth this book has something to offer all readers: a call to thoughtful reflection about how we can live our happiest lives, what our purpose is on earth, and how to be responsible, productive citizens of the world.

DISCUSSION/REFLECTION STRATEGIES

- The either/or situation posited by Anna Holmes recurs frequently in this collection. Is parenting truly an either/or situation, where mothers and fathers gain the fulfillment of having children but lose any hope of finding their authentic selves?

- Many contributors point out that probing questions about their decision to remain childless put them on the defensive. Recent census numbers show that about 50 percent of Americans under the age of forty-five are childless. Why, then, do we seem to automatically expect that everyone wants to have children and eventually will?

EXTRA CREDIT

One book that tackles the myth of "having it all" from the perspectives of personal experience and research is Anne-Marie Slaughter's *Unfinished Business: Women Men Work Family*. For a consideration of what it means to be a parent today, try Jennifer Senior's *All Joy and No Fun: The Paradox of Modern Parenting*.

CAN'T WE TALK ABOUT SOMETHING MORE PLEASANT?

Roz Chast

Can't We Talk about Something More Pleasant? is the funniest tragedy you'll ever read. It's a memoir of the years Chast, an only child, spends taking care of her elderly parents as they age into their nineties and begin inevitably to decline. So much goes unspoken in the Chast family (hence the title), and she and her parents have never talked about death, incapacitating illness, or any of the decisions that might need to be made at the end of her parents' lives. Chast is left to negotiate the unfamiliar territory of elder care with two parents who actively resist her attempts to keep them safe and reasonably well cared for.

Chast's memoir covers her parents' final years but also examines her own memories of growing up and the chronic unhappiness of her childhood home. Additionally, the book functions as an exposé of an industry that needs serious reform. Even more than that, Chast's book suggests the need to ask hard questions about our belief that staying alive for as long as possible is more important than anything else. Probably none of this sounds very funny, but Chast, well known for her *New Yorker* cartoons and covers, has a way of finding laugh-out-loud moments in the midst of anxiety and despair.

DISCUSSION/REFLECTION STRATEGIES

- One of the problems Chast faces is that her parents haven't spoken about their wishes and refuse to start. Maybe if they don't talk about death, it won't actually happen to them. Ideally, at what age do we need to have this talk with our parents or older family members? How can we create the space for such a conversation, and how can we continue once we begin?

- What do the drawings bring to the tale that would not be easy to do in pure prose? Or, conversely, why do you think careful reflection about the end of one's parents' lives is more suited to a traditional format?

- Have you been able to have these conversations with your own loved ones? What do you take away from this book that might change how you prepare for the years ahead?

EXTRA CREDIT

Atul Gawande's *Being Mortal: Medicine and What Matters in the End* is a natural follow-up read for those who want to think more deeply about the practical and philosophical issues about end-of-life care raised by Chast in *Can't We Talk about Something More Pleasant?*

Visit MichaelMaslin.com for a blog called *Ink Spill*, devoted to the works of cartoonists of the *New Yorker*.

PREGNANT BUTCH: NINE LONG MONTHS IN DRAG

A. K. Summers

Comics artist A. K. Summers fictionalizes her own experiences as a "pregnant butch" in this graphic novel about Teek Thomasson, a lesbian cartoonist who has decided to start a family with her partner, Vee. Both before and during her pregnancy, Teek is skeptical of the narrative that depicts pregnant women as glowing earth mamas, radiant with joy and fecundity. For Teek, pregnancy is mostly about indignity, discomfort, and gender confusion: she is a butch lesbian whose identity is closely tied to her masculine appearance. And no one, including Teek herself, quite knows what to do with a woman who looks like a man who also happens to have a giant pregnant belly.

Summers chronicles the challenges of pregnancy—a body that feels out of control, a partner who sometimes seems distant, worry about desirability, worry about the future—with wry humor and raw honesty.

DISCUSSION/REFLECTION STRATEGIES

- Summers describes pregnancy as a "performance." How could a physical experience like pregnancy be considered a performance? In what ways do you believe we perform masculinity and femininity?

- *Pregnant Butch* is about the specific identity issues that pregnancy creates for a butch lesbian, but it's also a story that anyone who's ever been pregnant—or ever known anyone who's been pregnant—can relate to and connect with. What aspects of pregnancy does Summers capture especially well?

Did You Know...?

Pregnant Butch was a finalist for the **Lambda Literary Award**, an annual award celebrating the best LGBTQ fiction and nonfiction stories. A complete list of finalists and winners can be found at LambdaLiterary.org/awards.

EXTRA CREDIT

For a very different graphic novel reading experience, try A. K. Summers's own favorite graphic novel of 2015, *This One Summer*, a poignant story by Mariko Tamaki and Jillian Tamaki about two tween girls trying to navigate their last summer on the brink of becoming teenagers. *This One Summer* won a Caldecott Honor Award for distinguished illustration and a Printz Honor Award for best book for teens.

Most books written about pregnancy tend to focus on nutrition and body changes, which is great, but the memoirs below talk about the personal experience: how life changes and how hard and beautiful that can be.

- *It Sucked and Then I Cried: How I Had a Baby, a Breakdown, and a Much Needed Margarita* by Heather Armstrong
- *The Room Lit by Roses: A Journal of Pregnancy and Birth* by Carol Maso
- *Operating Instructions: A Journal of My Son's First Year* by Anne Lamott
- *Guarding the Moon: A Mother's First Year* by Francesca Lia Block
- *A Life's Work: On Becoming a Mother* by Rachel Cusk

THE BEAUTIFUL STRUGGLE: A FATHER, TWO SONS, AND AN UNLIKELY ROAD TO MANHOOD

Ta-Nehisi Coates

The Beautiful Struggle is Ta-Nehisi Coates's memoir of growing up in inner-city Baltimore, the son of a former Black Panther determined to raise black sons to adulthood in a world that threatens their physical safety on a daily basis. And it's the story of two sons, Ta-Nehisi and his older brother, Bill, who inevitably try to make their own path in direct conflict with their parents' desires. There are mothers in this book too—four of them, in fact—who mother Ta-Nehisi and his siblings and half-siblings, but this is a book about boys being raised into a culture of manhood by other men.

And it's often brutal. Coates grows up in a neighborhood that's devastated by crack, gangs, crime. He learns the fear of those streets at a very young age. As a thoughtful boy who loves music, "[writes] rhymes at night," and doesn't want to fight, Coates struggles to figure out who he is and where he belongs. Coates's father, Paul, a man of strong opinions and ideals, tries to offer a different path through black revolutionary thinking. Coates realizes that much of what his father teaches is right in theory, but in practice, his father's different ideals are not a match for what Coates wants from his own life. How will Coates survive the "beautiful struggle" of growing up in this environment, in this family?

DISCUSSION/REFLECTION STRATEGIES

- While reading Coates's revelations about his father and mother, how do your understanding and values surrounding parenthood contract or expand? Other than his father, who are Coates's male role models?
- There is no question that his father's methods for raising his sons are unconventional and even extreme. Can you see advantages in his methods? If so, what are they?

- Coates has said that his mother married his father because she believed he would be a good father. How would she have defined "good father." How would you define it?

EXTRA CREDIT

For a female coming-of-age story set in a similar environment to *The Beautiful Struggle*, read Sheri Booker's *Nine Years Under: Coming of Age in an Inner-City Funeral Home*.

JOURNEYS

- *Kinky Gazpacho: Life, Love, and Spain* by Lori L. Tharps
- *We Mammals in Hospitable Times* by Jynne Dilling Martin
- *In the Land of Invisible Women: A Female Doctor's Journey in the Saudi Kingdom* by Qanta Ahmed
- *The Arrival* by Shaun Tan
- *The Painted Drum* by Louise Erdrich

In this month's selections, we look at books about people who travel out from their familiar environments to visit new territories. These journeys are not always comfortable, and the destinations don't always match the travelers' expectations. But these compelling stories convey a rich sense of the excitement that comes with striking forth into the unknown.

KINKY GAZPACHO: LIFE, LOVE, AND SPAIN

Lori L. Tharps

Lori Tharps's engaging and humorous memoir chronicles her rocky relationship with the country and culture of Spain. As a child, she became enamored of the language and knew somehow that Spain would be important to her in her life. The book covers her school life in Milwaukee, a high school trip to Morocco, a relationship with a Spanish exchange student, and her junior year abroad in Salamanca. There she meets a fellow student, falls in love, and eventually marries, the couple dividing their time between the United States and Spain. Tharps tells of her relationships with students, her family, and her husband's family with sharp insight and an eye for revealing detail.

But *Kinky Gazpacho* is also about much larger issues and how they play out in one person's life. Tharps spends her youth wondering who she is and where she belongs. As a child, Tharps is one of the few black students in her private school. A year in a public school sees her with other black students but made to feel uncomfortable for "talking white." In Morocco, it is her "Americanness" rather than her race that singles her out. At Smith College, she tries to join the Black Student Association but once again feels like an outsider. But it is in Spain, where jokes and comments directed at her are openly racist, that Tharps encounters her greatest challenge. Can she cultivate a relationship with the country she adores, the man she loves, and his family? Can living and loving in Spain provide her with the tools to carve out her own space and build a life of her own?

DISCUSSION/REFLECTION STRATEGIES

- There are times when Tharps is singled out because of her race, but other times she feels awkward for other reasons. Think about the various ways she is at odds with her surroundings. What are they and how does she cope? Would you have done the same?

- How does Tharps come to terms with her adopted country? What makes her feel better about being in Spain? How does researching Spanish history change her relationship to the culture? How does knowing the history of your country contribute to your sense of belonging?

- If you had to come up with a slogan for your relationship, like in *Kinky Gazpacho*, what would it be?

EXTRA CREDIT

Tharps is interested in hair—her own and other people's. She mentions how she wears her hair at different
times and places, talks about treatments and rituals, and
considers hair to be as much as an indicator of ethnicity
as skin color. Tharps's interest in hair and ethnicity gets
the full treatment in her book *Hair Story: Untangling the
Roots of Black Hair in America,* which is coauthored with
Ayana Byrd. This is a chronological look at the history
of hair treatments and styles of Black Americans from
fifteenth-century Africa to the present day.

Sociologist Althea Prince also writes on the topic in her
The Politics of Black Women's Hair. Prince interviews
women from the U.S., the UK, the Caribbean, and
South America, getting multiple perspectives on how
people feel about their hair and how those feelings are
communicated across generations.

WE MAMMALS IN HOSPITABLE TIMES

Jynne Dilling Martin

In 2013, Jynne Dilling Martin was selected as an Antarctic Artist in Residence, a program supported by the National Science Foundation that sends an artist or writer to Antarctica for six weeks to live, work, and be creatively inspired by the earth's least hospitable environment. Many of the poems in *We Mammals in Hospitable Times* reflect her experiences there. These poems do not always address Antarctica directly, but Martin's reflections on time, stillness, and the connections and mysteries of nature that emerge from insights and observations made during her Antarctic sojourn. Many of these poems are dark, positing a future of ecological devastation mostly caused by humans, but many of them are also very funny. Animals feature prominently, from house cats who run from the vacuum cleaner to sea turtles who must inhale and exhale only three times a day. Martin's keen eye for detail and sharp turn of phrase create memorable images and lines that will linger long after you close this volume.

DISCUSSION/REFLECTION STRATEGIES

- Many readers find it difficult to respond to poetry, but poetry can be enormously rewarding. Ask yourself these questions as you read a poem:
    - What does the poem seem to be about?
    - What pictures form in your mind as you're reading?
    - What lines, pictures, or phrases stand out, and how do they relate to the overall meaning?
    - How does the title relate to the poem?
- Even a weekend camping trip can test us if it is not something we normally do. What's the most unusual place you've ever been or the most arduous journey you've ever had? What were the challenges you faced, and how did you feel at the end of it?

Did You Know...?

The National Science Foundation features a list of the Antarctic Artists and Writers Program partici- pants, with links to their books, films, art projects, and other works at nsf.gov.

EXTRA CREDIT

If you like reading about Antarctica, then you will like *Skating to Antarctica* by Jenni Diski, first published in 1998. Diski writes a straightforward account of trav- eling to Antarctica in order to "write white," the color of oblivion for Diski. It's also an account of trying to dissuade her daughter from looking for Diski's mother, who disappeared from her life in 1966.

Accounts of Antarctica are also always stories about silence. *A Book of Silence,* by Sara Maitland, tells of the author's desire to live in pure silence and to find the spiritual benefits to be gathered from that state. This is a brief history of silence as well, where she tells of hermits and explorers and what they discover when there is nothing to hear.

IN THE LAND OF INVISIBLE WOMEN: A FEMALE DOCTOR'S JOURNEY IN THE SAUDI KINGDOM

Qanta Ahmed

In this mesmerizing and important memoir, Qanta Ahmed shares what it is like to be a doctor, a woman, and a Western Muslim in Saudi Arabia. Ahmed lived in the kingdom for several years starting in the late 1990s, working in a hospital after completing training in the United States. As a woman in Saudi Arabia, she is not allowed to drive and cannot go out in public without wearing an *abbaya*—a floor-length garment that also covers her hair. If her hair shows, even accidentally, she is likely to be accosted by the

Mutawaeen, the religious police. Ahmed writes candidly and vividly about her work in the hospital as one of the few female doctors in the country. She describes going on the hajj, the pilgrimage to the sacred city of Mecca, and how her commitment to Islam deepens even as she deplores certain aspects of Saudi interpretation of Islamic law.

If you are not familiar with Islam as it is lived by its many practitioners, this book is an excellent place to start learning. If you are familiar with Islam, you will still find Dr. Ahmed's account of life in Saudi riveting.

DISCUSSION/REFLECTION STRATEGIES

- Have you ever lived in a place or belonged to an institution that curtailed some of the freedoms you take for granted (for example, living in a monastery, going on a silent retreat, being in the military)? If so, how did you adapt? If you haven't, could you live in someplace like Saudi Arabia? Think about the strictures placed on women and men in the kingdom. What would be most difficult for you?

- If you are Muslim or acquainted with Islam, how does Ahmed's account of her spiritual journey resonate with you? What about the distinctions she draws between Islam and the interpretation of it by the Wahabi? If you were raised in another religious tradition, do you see any parallels between your beliefs and practices and those described by Ahmed?

- Think about the reaction to 9/11 as Ahmed observed it in Saudi Arabia. What are some of the reasons people expressed approval for what happened, and how did they make you feel? This is a difficult topic to discuss, but it is really worth doing. Take a deep breath and think about why reactions to 9/11 could vary so widely.

- Ahmed has to wear the *abbaya* in Saudi Arabia because it is the law. Think about modern clothing for women and men in the West. Are there any things that you wear that you would rather not? Probably, no one is threatening you with arrest if you do not wear certain clothes, such as high heels, but do you feel (or have you ever felt) any social pressure to wear them? We like to think we make our own choices about these things, but how are our choices modified by social demands?

EXTRA CREDIT

If you enjoyed *In the Land of Invisible Women*, you might try Patrick Notestine's *Paramedic to the Prince: An American Paramedic's Account of Life Inside the Mysterious World of the Kingdom of Saudi Arabia*. The author spent ten years working on the medical staff of the Saudi King.

THE ARRIVAL

Shaun Tan

∾

The Arrival is probably unlike any other reading experience you've had. It's a wordless graphic novel whose entire story is told through images. There is not even an author's note, introduction, or afterword to guide readers! Most readers associate reading with processing text, and the shift from text to image can be tricky, as Shaun Tan fully understands. Going wordless is a brilliant choice to disorient his reader, much as his characters, immigrants to a world that is literally alien, are disoriented by their new experiences. The unnamed main character leaves his family early in the story to move to a new land where he's confronted by many unknowns—language, money, food, weather, animals, clothing, customs. He meets other immigrants who share their stories in poignant illustrated sequences that capture the fear, uncertainty, and loss experienced by those who leave their home cultures and lands for new worlds.

The Arrival raises questions about belonging and identity and about how to find a place for ourselves in a world that feels foreign and strange.

DISCUSSION/REFLECTION STRATEGIES

- One challenge of reading *The Arrival* is navigating wordless text and gleaning information and meaning solely from images. Many readers report the need to read much more slowly and carefully and to check their comprehension by "rereading" certain portions of the text. Do you have a special strategy that you use when you read *The Arrival*?

- If you are reading this with a group, have any of you come up with different interpretations of what is happening? Shaun Tan explains on his website that *The Arrival* is specifically a story about immigration and the experience of being a refugee. What clues in the story helped you understand this?

Did You Know...?

Shaun Tan's *Arrival* may be the best-known wordless graphic novel, but it's actually part of a long tradition dating back to Belgian artist Franz Masereel, who created what's considered the first wordless novel in 1918. Masereel's work influenced later artists in Germany who worked extensively with sequences of woodcuts to tell wordless stories. The tradition passed to America via artist Lynd Ward, who studied art in Leipzig in 1926 and made the form his own by engraving wood rather than using woodcutting techniques. Ward's books influenced pioneering graphic novelist Will Eisner, whose book *A Contract with God and Other Tenement Stories* is considered by some to be the first modern graphic novel.

EXTRA CREDIT

If you think that Tan's sepia-toned sketches resemble old photographs, you're right. Photographs of immigrants at Ellis Island were a main source of research and inspiration for him. Search for "Ellis Island" at the Library of Congress website, loc.gov.

Louise Erdrich

Faye Travers lives in a small New England town with her mother. Together they run a business appraising estates and selling antiques. Faye is happy enough with her life; she likes her job, loves her mother, has a lover who doesn't pressure her too much. And if she doesn't reflect too much on her past or feel much enthusiasm for her present, well, she does not see that as a problem. While on a job, Faye finds an old, perfectly crafted, and ornately decorated Ojibwe drum. She feels an immediate connection to it and is driven to find out where it came from. Discovering the drum's journey and the people from whom it was taken forces Faye to reflect on her own journey—her relationships, her own past, and the past of her people.

This is a hypnotic novel that draws on voices of many characters, living and dead. As in most Louise Erdrich novels, the line between the physical world and spirit world is semipermeable. Erdrich's novels are rich, detailed, and so compelling that the reader ends up looking at her own world more closely and questioning commonplace distinctions between body and spirit.

DISCUSSION/REFLECTION STRATEGIES

- Think about the families in this novel. What, in your opinion, makes a strong, good family? Several of the families are troubled, yet their affection for one another remains strong. What are the ties that bind troubled families? Why do people in these families honor those ties despite all the troubles?

- The relationships between mothers and daughters are featured prominently in *The Painted Drum*, as does the notion of forgiveness. In your experience, how does forgiveness play a role in relationships between mothers and daughters (or parents and children)?

- Erdrich mentions in the afterword of the novel that the story of the girl lost to the wolves is one that shows up in many places, notably Willa Cather's *My Ántonia*. As shocking as the story is, explain why you are, or you are not, convinced by the alternative reading of the tragedy given by Bernard Shaawano.

Did You Know...?

The Ojibwe language makes a fundamental grammatical distinction between animate and inanimate objects, and drums are classified as animate objects. The Anishinaabe Ojibwe consider the drum to be a mode of transmitting messages from the collective voice of the physical world to the spirit world. Master craftsmen frequently make drums after visionary experiences. Drums are accorded great respect, kept wrapped in blankets, and periodically presented with offerings of tobacco and sage. To find out more about drums in Ojibwe life, visit pluralism .org. If you are interested in seeing Ojibwe drums in action, YouTube is a great place to start.

August

STARTING OVER

- *The Best of All Possible Worlds* by Karen Lord
- *The Fifth Season* by N. K. Jemisin
- *Gold Fame Citrus* by Claire Vaye Watkins
- *The Summer Prince* by Alaya Dawn Johnson
- *Station Eleven* by Emily St. John Mandel

If this month had a theme song, it would be R.E.M.'s "It's the End of the World As We Know It." In each of these post-apocalyptic novels, the survivors must start over, often without key necessities like adequate water, food, or electricity. Although these novels might seem speculative, they also raise thoughtful questions about the ways we live now.

THE BEST OF ALL POSSIBLE WORLDS

Karen Lord

The Sadiri are a race of humans nearly wiped out in an interplanetary battle that has made their home planet uninhabitable. The few surviving Sadiri, those who were off-planet at the time of the attack, are forced to try to rebuild their numbers and their culture on Cygnus Beta—a planet made up of descendants of refugees from various intergalactic conflicts. The Sadiri are a proud people whose gifts include telepathy and adherence to a rigid moral code. They are grateful for the chance to rebuild on Cygnus Beta, but at times they find the polyglot communities of the planet incompatible with their own way of life.

Grace Delarua is a civil servant for the governing body of Cygnus Beta assigned as a liaison to the Sadiri to facilitate their integration into society. Grace, a biologist and linguist, is fascinated by the Sadiri. Grace has a troubled past which, despite her efforts to suppress it, surfaces in her relationship with the Sadiri.

This is a novel with some classic science fiction elements: space travel, time travel, and telepathy. But it is more than a series of exotic happenings. It is about how a people can begin again after catastrophe. How can the Sadiri honor their dead loved ones and their destroyed planet while at the same time moving forward into new ways of life? How can Grace overcome her traumatic history and learn to love and live again?

DISCUSSION/REFLECTION STRATEGIES

- Science fiction novels are at their best when the conundrums facing the characters are familiar to those facing readers. It's not all about the rocket ships and the strange landscapes. Dllenahkh is a refugee trying to keep his people safe and his culture alive. Grace is suffering from the aftermath of an abusive relationship and trying to keep her family safe. How else do Dllenahkh's and Grace's stories mirror one another? Do their respective stories resonate with what you know about life after tragedy? How do people move on, and does anyone ever really "begin again"?

Did You Know...?

Karen Lord chose as the title of her novel a phrase coined by German philosopher Gottfried Leibniz in 1710. Leibniz was working on what philosophers call "the problem of evil," i.e., If God is all-knowing, all-powerful, and good, then how can evil exist? It seems that for evil to exist, God would have to be either not all-knowing or not all-powerful or not good. Christian orthodoxy insists that God is all three. Hence the problem. Leibniz maintained that yes, God is all good, all-powerful, and all-knowing. According to Leibniz, God's goodness guarantees that such evil as there is in the world is the minimum consistent with the greater good of human free will.

EXTRA CREDIT

If you are intrigued by the problem of evil and want to read more, find a copy of the Bible and read the book of Job. It is a great place to start.

— — — — — — — — — —

THE FIFTH SEASON

N. K. Jemisin

In *The Fifth Season*, the first novel in N. K. Jemisin's *Broken Earth* trilogy, the world is in constant upheaval from earthquakes, volcanoes, and other natural disasters, and its citizens can only try to survive day to day, knowing that every few hundred years, the entire world explodes. Jemisin's interesting twist is that some people in this world are able to control or influence the elements of the earth—rock, fire, water— through the powers of their mind. But they are feared by many, hunted, persecuted, even killed.

The novel weaves together three plots, but as is fitting in the first volume of a trilogy, the three story lines don't fully converge yet. There is Essun, a woman who has just lost her son and embarks on a quest for revenge and in search of her daughter. There is Damaya, a young girl whose powers have just been revealed and whose parents send her away for her own protection. And there is Syenite, who has just graduated from the magic academy and is ready to use her powers for good.

The world Jemisin builds is complex, wild, and dangerous, though it is not without beauty and wonder as well. As in much postapocalyptic fantasy, where "nature versus man" is a major theme, it is really the injustices created by humanity that bring daily hardship and woe to all. Like all good stories ever told, even ones about the end of the world, *The Fifth Season* is really about personal discovery, emotional relationships, and the journey of living.

DISCUSSION/REFLECTION STRATEGIES

- How does Jemisin make readers engage with her characters and their plights?
- Postapocalyptic fantasy can be a dark reading experience. Television shows and movies often focus on catastrophe and its aftermath. Why do you think it is a popular theme? Why might people be drawn to these books and shows? How do you think you would cope under similar circumstances?

Did You Know...?

Both fantasy and science fiction are examples of what is called **speculative literature**. The terms are not interchangeable, though it is not always easy to tell if a book is a work of fantasy or of science fiction, because the genres often overlap. The term **fantasy** generally refers to works of literature that employ imaginary worlds peopled by supernatural or mythical beings. In these works, impossible things may happen (impossible in our world, anyway), but no scientific explanation is given. In **science fiction**, stories are usually set in the future, and plots tend to rely on particular aspects of science and/or technology. For example, an author may create an entire culture living on another planet, but may explain features of that culture as resulting from characteristics of the planet's atmosphere or geography.

EXTRA CREDIT

N. K. Jemisin writes a bimonthly book review column called "Otherworldly" for the *New York Times*. Her column is a terrific resource for speculative literature book recommendations.

Claire Vaye Watkins

⌇

Gold Fame Citrus imagines the barren landscape and human desperation that result after water sources dry up in the Western United States and most of the Southwest turns into a punishing desert. The gold, fame, and citrus of the title situate us firmly in southern California. The story opens with Luz, a former model who has taken up residence with her boyfriend, Ray, a former soldier who suffers from PTSD. Many of Los Angeles's inhabitants have either died or fled the city; the people who are left make up ragtag bands of criminal and lunatics. The plot kicks into high gear when Ray and Luz are forced to leave the city after kidnapping a neglected toddler named Ig. They don't have the resources to raise a baby, but Luz is convinced they can do a better job than this little girl's strung-out abusive family. Their road trip quickly stalls in the vast desert that now surrounds Los Angeles, and the rest of the novel explores how people who were probably already living on the fringe before the apocalypse cope in such extreme and desperate circumstances.

Survival does not bring out the best in anyone in *Gold Fame Citrus*. There are no heroes in Watkins's postapocalyptic world, only flawed people trying to cope, often badly. Watkins's lush prose creates an eerie, disorienting atmosphere that is a huge part of the appeal of this story.

DISCUSSION/REFLECTION STRATEGIES

- Like so many postapocalyptic novels set in the future, *Gold Fame Citrus* reflects concerns that clearly connect to this moment. How likely does Watkins's drought-ridden scenario seem to you, and why?

- Watkins's book raises interesting questions about the strength of relationships in times of survival. What roles do our significant relationships play in our ability to recover after disaster? When survival is at stake, how do these intense times affect our relationships?

- Emily St. John Mandel reviewed this book for the

New York Times Book Review and said that the novel is as much about the "dark side of celebrity culture" as anything else. Explore this idea. Where in the text do you see this at work?

Did You Know...?

Allegory is the literary term for a narrative that has a literal, primary meaning, but also a metaphorical, secondary meaning. That is, the narrative, while literally representing one event or character, is actually alluding to something else. George Orwell's *Animal Farm* is one good example.

EXTRA CREDIT

Claire Vaye Watkins took the Internet by storm with the publication of "On Pandering," an essay on what it's like to be a woman writing and publishing literary fiction in a misogynist culture that devalues not only women's writing but women themselves. The essay went viral and sparked considerable conversation on social media. You can access the essay at TinHouse.com.

Alaya Dawn Johnson

This is a young adult novel and one with enough action, complex characters, and moral questions to engage readers of all ages. Rising from the ashes of environmental catastrophe, the new Brazilian city of Palmares Tres fuses technology and tradition. Amazing advances coexist with ancient (and perhaps misremembered) practices, such as human sacrifice. June Costa is seventeen years old and already an accomplished artist in Palmares Tres. She spends her time hanging out with her best friend, Gil, and creating new art projects. June doesn't really question her society until she and Gil both fall in love with Enki, who is selected as the Summer King. This coveted position gives him the power to help rule the city and select the next queen, but it also comes with a price: at the end of his year, he will be sacrificed for the safety and continuation of the city.

June, Gil, and Enki fuel the growing discontent in the city toward the oppressive regime that rules it. Can the friends survive life in this futuristic hell? Can they build a new city based on freedom?

DISCUSSION/REFLECTION STRATEGIES

- Like historical novels, futuristic fiction often reflects the concerns of the author's present. Setting the novel at a temporal distance allows authors to reflect and comment on contemporary issues with freedom and ingenuity. Given that, what concerns, present in our world today, is Johnson talking about in *The Summer Prince*?

- June frequently uses her status as an artist to justify her behavior. A lot of the work that she and Enki produce also serves their political activism goals. Can art be political, and should it be? What is art to you?

- There is a division in the text between those who demand more technology and those who want to suppress innovation. Where do you stand on this issue? Most of us are neither one nor the other. But how do you navigate the enormous technological changes we've all witnessed in our lives?

Did You Know...?

The city in *The Summer Prince,* Palmares Tres, is named after a seventeenth-century settlement of fugitive slaves in northeastern Brazil called Palmares. Numbering 20,000 inhabitants at its height, Palmares was the largest and longest lasting runaway slave community in Brazil. It was founded in 1604 and finally suppressed in 1694.

In addition to escaped African slaves, fugitive communities called *quilombos* also provided refuge to Indians and poor whites, especially Portuguese soldiers escaping from the military. Numerous *quilombos* existed in Brazil, and they were considered a serious threat to the existing social order.

☀ EXTRA CREDIT ☀

If you're interested in the intersection between art and politics have a look at the work of British-born (but otherwise anonymous) graffiti artist Banksy. Check out Banksy.co.uk. For more on Banksy and modern art, see the film *Exit through the Gift Shop*.

— — — — — — — — —

STATION ELEVEN

Emily St. John Mandel

ℓ

If there's such a thing as a sweet postapocalyptic novel, *Station Eleven* is it. Certainly life is no easier for Mandel's characters than for most characters in novels about the end of the world, but most of Mandel's characters retain humanity, generosity of spirit, curiosity about the world, and hopefulness that gets lost or forgotten in most postapocalyptic stories. Perhaps it's because so many of the characters in *Station Eleven* are creative—actors and musicians in a traveling troupe of performers who journey from town to town, staging plays and concerts for the survivors of the Georgia Flu. Perhaps it's because *Station Eleven* is set fifteen years after a major catastrophe: it's only natural for the world to "soften" and move into rebuilding mode when survival seems more likely. Nevertheless, there is much that is sinister and threatening for these characters, especially after they visit a town called St. Deborah by the Water and have a run-in with the local "prophet," a charismatic extremist who controls the town's inhabitants through intimidation, fear-mongering, and polygamy.

The narrative structure of *Station Eleven* is one of its most innovative and engaging features. The story moves between pre- and postapocalypse, and the connections among characters and plots only gradually become clear to the reader.

DISCUSSION/REFLECTION STRATEGIES

- When we read postapocalyptic novels, we become caught up in a hope that things will work out in spite of what the book's characters have to endure. As you read *Station Eleven*, what are you imagining as the best possible outcome?

- Mandel's novel and others in this genre suggest that at some point in the future, we may have to start over. How easily would you be able to adapt to a life focused on survival? How could we ensure a better outcome than the one offered in so many postapocalyptic novels?

Did You Know...?

Station Eleven appeared on dozens of "Best Books of the Year" lists compiled and published by book reviews, magazines, and newspapers. These annual lists are excellent places to discover high-quality literature. We especially like lists by the *Guardian*, *Kirkus Reviews*, and the *Huffington Post*. Most lists try to limit the quantity of "best books" to ten, but if ten isn't enough, try the one hundred titles on Amazon's annual "Editors' Picks" list.

EXTRA CREDIT

Check out *The World without Us* by Alan Weisman. This speculative nonfiction book explores what would happen to the planet if humans were wiped out by some kind of disaster.

September

THIS DIGITAL LIFE

- *Reclaiming Conversation: The Power of Talk in a Digital Age*
  by Sherry Turkle
- *So You've Been Publicly Shamed* by Jon Ronson
- *The Circle* by Dave Eggers
- *The Boy Kings: A Journey into the Heart of the Social Network*
  by Katherine Losse
- *In Real Life* by Cory Doctorow and Jen Wang

This month, we examine the brave new world of social media and online activity. These titles explore the impact that our digital lives have on our real lives. The news isn't all good: our relationships, our attention spans, and possibly our very humanity itself may be threatened by the choices we make in our digital lives. But there is a lot of hope here as well in the potential of digital technology to help us make connections and improve our world.

RECLAIMING CONVERSATION: THE POWER OF TALK IN A DIGITAL AGE

Sherry Turkle

Media scholar Sherry Turkle has spent many years charting the ways digital technology has changed human behavior. In *Reclaiming Conversation* she explores our dependence on social media and examines what so much screen time is doing to us as individuals, as people in relationships, and as members of the larger community. The argument is simple and not unfamiliar: our dependence on screens may increase our connection with the world, but it actually diminishes the depth of our connection with our friends, family, and even ourselves. Turkle notes that she is not "anti-technology but pro-conversation." Face-to-face conversation, it turns out, is largely what teaches us empathy and compassion. Even the boredom that we currently avoid by pulling out a device has its uses: it is in facing boredom and having genuine downtime (not empty time filled with surfing the Internet) that we establish a relationship with ourselves. The quality of our relationship with ourselves ultimately allows us to have deeper relationships with other people.

DISCUSSION/REFLECTION STRATEGIES

- At the beginning of the chapter titled "Solitude," Turkle quotes the comedian Louis C.K. at length on why he will not allow his children to have cell phones. Read the quotation again, for it is a vivid, funny, and sad summary of Turkle's own argument on boredom and emotions. How do you find yourself using your screen to avoid boredom and strong emotions? What are the benefits of feelings like sadness, embarrassment, or shame?

- Turkle tells the story of parents whose son has a standing dinner invitation with his grandparents each week. The boy does not always want to go, but his parents tell him that if he wishes to cancel, he has to call his grandparents on the phone and tell them. He is not allowed to email or text them. How does a phone call help build empathy in a way that texting or emailing doesn't?

EXTRA CREDIT

Turkle points to research that concludes that reading literary fiction improves the ability to empathize. OK, if you are reading this book, you must think that reading, discussing, and thinking about literature is a worthwhile thing to do. Do you think reading literary fiction helps to make you a better person? Why do you get together to talk about books with others, and how are book group discussions held in person different from those held online?

– – – – – – – – – –

SO YOU'VE BEEN PUBLICLY SHAMED

Jon Ronson

Jon Ronson's wide-ranging book explores what feels like a new cultural phenomenon: public shaming on social media. His journey to understand who gets publicly shamed and why, and how these people cope after losing friends, jobs, and their public reputation, takes him to some unusual places, including a Radical Honesty workshop and a porn film set. Much of his time, however, is spent interviewing the victims of public shaming, and he uses the word "victim" advisedly: it's difficult not to think of many of those profiled in his book as victims. Their misstatement or ill-advised joke or comment goes viral, and they find themselves targeted by millions of outraged strangers who comment on the transgression, from the mild "Wow, that was stupid" to really graphic and disturbing death threats made directly to the perpetrators of the so-called crime.

Ronson notes that most of the transgressions that outrage the public—a juvenile penis joke overheard at a tech conference, a sarcastic tweet that comes across as racist—have no victims: they are not evil acts that actually hurt anyone. Why, then, do we become so furious with those who "misspeak"? Why do we feel comfortable attacking strangers on the Internet and calling—sometimes literally!—for their heads? *So You've Been Publicly Shamed* invites us to reconsider the culture we're creating on social media and to take action on instilling empathy and forgiveness into that culture.

DISCUSSION/REFLECTION STRATEGIES

- Ronson may be advocating for a new behavior code specific to social media based on courtesy and respect toward others. What three rules of behavior do you believe could cover all potential transgressions, or do you believe three rules are too few or too many?

- Ronson examines many different possible responses to public shaming. Which responses seem the most effective and healthy to you?

EXTRA CREDIT

Monica Lewinsky knows a thing or two about public shame, and she shares insights from her experiences and advocates for more kindness and compassion in social media environments in her TED Talk, "The Price of Shame." Brené Brown is a social scientist and researcher who studies shame and urges viewers to confront shame head-on in her TED Talk, "Listening to Shame."

THE CIRCLE

Dave Eggers

ℓ

Twenty-four-year-old Mae is thrilled to be working for the world's most successful corporation, the Circle, which combines all the features of Google, Facebook, Twitter, and Instagram into one seamless whole. The company has revolutionized the Internet through technological advances that eliminate the need for passwords, anonymity, and log-ins: everyone has one username (which is their real name) and secure access to all websites. The Circle employees work on a gorgeous campus with access to every service and entertainment they could possibly want: shopping, health care, exhaustive recreational facilities, endless parties. The work is demanding but prestigious and well paid. Mae, who has grown up in a lower-middle-class town with parents who struggled to make ends meet, is awestruck by the opportunity to make decent money, be a trendsetter, and even get good health care for her parents.

Of course, things are not so rosy as they seem. As we follow Mae throughout her workday, we see that transparency and nonstop community come at a high price. Mae is presented with an increasingly bizarre set of life choices that reveal the downside of the principles that she and her fellow employees have adopted. The notion of privacy in particular is denigrated. "Privacy is theft" is one of the corporation's catchphrases. But who needs privacy when you have nothing to hide and happiness is guaranteed?

DISCUSSION REFLECTION/STRATEGY

- Would you work for the Circle? Think about your own relationship to social media. How do you participate? If you don't participate, do you feel that you are missing out? How do you navigate privacy concerns on different platforms?

Did You Know...?

In her essay on *The Circle* for the *New York Review of Books*, novelist Margaret Atwood refers to the novel as a Menippean satire. A **Menippean satire** is a novel of ideas rather than a character-driven novel. The protagonist in a novel of ideas may not be a fully formed, three-dimensional character; rather, he or she could be considered a foil or a stand-in for the reader. Other novels that are characterized as Menippean satires include *Candide* by Voltaire, *The Hitchhiker's Guide to the Galaxy* by Douglas Adams, and *Gulliver's Travels* by Jonathan Swift.

THE BOY KINGS: A JOURNEY INTO THE HEART OF THE SOCIAL NETWORK

Katherine Losse

Katherine Losse is an early employee at Facebook, or "The Facebook," as it was originally known. She is hired to answer customer inquiries like "What does 'poke' mean?" or "Why has my friend blocked me?" From the beginning of her time at the company, she is simultaneously thrilled to be a part of something so exciting, with such potential for positive social change, but also nervous about certain aspects of the company culture. Eager to share the community that Facebook promised, she can't help but wonder why no one worries too much about the sexism, racism, and homophobia that show up on Facebook pages.

During her time at Facebook, Losse goes from customer support to the international team, where her job is to help roll out Facebook to different countries. She finally ends up as support assistant and ghostwriter to Mark Zuckerberg himself. Losse's memoir is a well-observed exploration of a global phenomenon written from an insider's perspective. Her account of the rise of Facebook will have you looking at the social media platform a bit differently.

DISCUSSION/REFLECTION STRATEGIES

- Losse delineates many problems with Facebook's internal structure and management culture. What are those problems, according to the author?
- Losse accuses the company of deliberately adopting the model of an elite school fraternity house in its disdain for the conventional, its mandatory *bonhomie*, and its certainty in the rightness of its own mission. In other words, Losse argues that Facebook staff never question what they are doing and why; they simply assume that whatever they do is all for the best. What are some of the shortcomings of this approach?

If you are a longtime Facebook user, have you seen developments that have made you question the enterprise?

EXTRA CREDIT

If you like *The Boy Kings*, have a look at *The Circle* by Dave Eggers, also featured in this chapter. It is an interesting comparison, though *The Circle* is fiction and *The Boy Kings* is not. How similar are the books? How are the protagonists the same in each book? How do they differ? How does Katherine Losse deal with her misgivings about the organization?

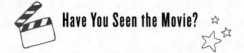 **Have You Seen the Movie?** ☆

The Oscar-winning 2010 film *The Social Network*, starring Jesse Eisenberg as Mark Zuckerberg, is a must-watch after reading this book. Critics rave about the film's ability to bring computer programming and financial deals to life. Compare the vision of Facebook shown in the film with Katherine Losse's memoir. How are they similar and how do they differ? The film is adapted from the book *The Accidental Billionaires: The Founding of Facebook* by Ben Mezrich, which is also worth a read.

Cory Doctorow and Jen Wang

Global economics, labor, and politics may not sound like the most obvious topics for a graphic novel published for young adults, but author Cory Doctorow packages his themes of social justice and global wealth inequity in a plot that has much more immediate teen appeal: the world of MMORPGs, massively multiplayer online role-playing games. The teenaged protagonist, Anda, loves online role-playing games. She's recruited to join an online guild dedicated to increasing the presence of women in the online gaming world. Anda discovers that wealthy Western players who don't want to put in the time and effort to "level up" in the game pay real-world currency to buy game currency that boosts their avatar. Persuaded that "gold farming" compromises the integrity of the game, Anda is hired by another player to go on "missions" to kill the gold farmers.

Little does she realize that there are real-world consequences to her actions in the game. Doctorow treats politics with a light touch, but it's not hard to see the cheats and shortcuts used by wealthy Western game players as a metaphor for the exploitation of poor nations by richer nations. Doctorow's story raises interesting questions about the nature of online participation and Internet activism. Jen Wang's eye-popping illustrations add immensely to the appeal of this story.

DISCUSSION/REFLECTION STRATEGIES

- In the introduction, Cory Doctorow claims that the Internet solves "the first hard problem of righting wrongs"—making connections between people and getting the word out about crises. In what ways does the Internet support Anda's growing under-standing of economics and worker exploitation, and how do you find her awakening believable?

- You may wish to read Doctorow's original short story, "Anda's Game," the source material for *In Real Life*, and compare the two. How does the experience of reading the story in a graphic novel format differ from reading it as prose fiction? Doctorow's short story is available online at his website.

EXTRA CREDIT

For an academic look at the topics Doctorow covers in *In Real Life*, read Edward Castranova's *Synthetic Worlds: The Business and Culture of Online Games*. Castranova, a professor at Indiana University, examines the economic and social ramifications of online gaming and argues that gaming-world economies are, in fact, real economies. For a more personal, essayistic look at video games as a pastime and art form, try Tom Bissell's *Extra Lives: Why Video Games Matter*.

October

READING ABOUT READING

- *All Roads Lead to Austen: A Yearlong Journey with Jane* by Amy Elizabeth Smith
- *Fangirl* by Rainbow Rowell
- *Good Night, Mr. Wodehouse* by Faith Sullivan
- *Reading Lolita in Tehran: A Memoir in Books* by Azar Nafisi
- *The World Between Two Covers: Reading the Globe* by Ann Morgan

For October, we go meta and read about reading. Just as foodies enjoy reading about food, it makes sense that the bookish would enjoy books about books. These titles explore the different ways that reading and books enrich and even change lives.

ALL ROADS LEAD TO AUSTEN: A YEARLONG JOURNEY WITH JANE

Amy Elizabeth Smith

This is an exuberant memoir about the joy of reading Jane Austen. Amy Smith, a literature professor at a university in California, loves teaching Jane Austen's novels to her mostly American students, and her students respond enthusiastically, even writing fan fiction based on Austen's works. Smith wonders how Austen's language of love, courtship, and class might appeal to readers from other cultures. Although she has limited Spanish language skills, she decides to travel to six Latin American countries to meet with book clubs and discuss Spanish translations of Austen's novels. The unique perspectives that Smith's Latin American book clubs bring to discussions of Austen's works illuminate these novels in new ways.

Smith writes in a breezy style, but there is a lot of depth to her memoir and a lot of information to process about the different Latin American countries she visits. In most of the countries she visits, poverty and deprivation rule people's lives. Can Smith and her interlocutors find common ground in Austen? And does Smith actually find her own Mr. Darcy on this trip?

DISCUSSION/REFLECTION STRATEGIES

- How do the reading groups Smith facilitates differ from one another? What conversations emerge from clubs in different countries and cultures?
- All the Austen heroines discover something about themselves over the course of the novels. What does Smith learn about herself in this journey, and which Austen heroine (if any) does she most remind you of?

EXTRA CREDIT

This memoir is not just about bringing Jane Austen to Central and South America. It is also about Smith learning about the literature from the countries she visits. If you enjoyed this glimpse into Latin America, you may enjoy reading some of its books. If you haven't read anything by Isabel Allende, stop what you're doing and get ahold of *The House of the Spirits*. Take a look at Che Guevara's *Motorcycle Diaries* (mentioned in Smith's book), the revolutionary's classic account of his long journey throughout South America, which opened his eyes to the endemic poverty and oppression of the region. Smith also mentions *Pedro Páramo* by Juan Rulfo, poorly received when it was published in Mexico in 1955, but now considered an influential masterpiece. A challenging read, but worth the effort, is *The Savage Detectives*, by Roberto Bolaño from Chile.

Rainbow Rowell

Cath Avery, a freshman at the University of Nebraska, is a prolific, popular author of fan fiction. Using the fictional world and characters of the extremely popular Simon Snow series (Simon Snow is a boy magician who goes to a school for young magicians and spends his time battling evil magicians—sound familiar?), Cath writes intense alternative adventures for the characters. She posts them online and has a significant following.

Her twin sister, Wren, used to write stories

with her, but has been distancing herself from fan fiction, and even from Cath herself. Without her sister, Cath is terrified at school. She does not know where anything is, she does not like meeting new people, and she's having roommate issues. When Cath fails an assignment in her fiction-writing class, she's ready to pack it all in and go home to Omaha to spend all her time writing about Simon Snow.

This coming-of-age novel is a book for teens. It is also a book for any reader who has ever been the new kid on the block or ever felt awkward around others. It's for people whose relationships have changed over time and who have made tentative steps toward intimacy with new people in their lives. Can Cath find it in herself to make new friends and maybe, just maybe, write about something else besides Simon Snow?

DISCUSSION/REFLECTION STRATEGIES

- How can we see Cath's growth over the year in her "relationship" to Simon Snow? How does her fan fiction writing change?

- What is your opinion of fan fiction? How much creativity do you think is involved, and what do you think people get from writing and reading it?

- Though styles may change, feeling out of place at school is an almost universal phenomenon. How did Cath's first few months at college resonate for you?

Did You Know...?

Cath Avery may be a fictional character, but writing **fan fiction** is very much an activity in the real world. There is a large and active subculture online writing and reading in the Harry Potter universe and in other fictional worlds as well, like *Star Wars* and *Star Trek*. In writing about a romantic relationship between Simon and Bas, Cath is writing in a subgenre of fanfic called **slash fiction**, which imagines romantic or sexual relationships between same-sex characters in a fictional world. Several well-known authors, such as Meg Cabot, S. E. Hinton, and Neil Gaiman, also write fan fiction.

EXTRA CREDIT

We strongly recommend that, at least once a year, book groups have a special meeting where each member invites a partner, friend, or family member to take part. Make it a party and assign a book that's accessible to different ages and interests. We think *Fangirl* is a terrific selection for an open meeting. Topics to discuss include: what it means to be a fan; what it means to be obsessed (have you ever had to draw back a bit from an intense fictional interest?); what it is like to go away from home for the first time. What is it like to try to fit in to a new environment?

GOOD NIGHT, MR. WODEHOUSE

Faith Sullivan

Good Night, Mr. Wodehouse opens with the obituary of the main character, which she writes herself fifteen years before she dies. In her obituary, Nell lists the main events of her life—a life which some may call small and ordinary. She is a wife, a mother, a teacher, a widow, a lover, and a friend to many. Throughout her life, Nell is also a reader who turns to novels for solace, entertainment, spiritual and intellectual growth. She is particularly devoted to the works of P. G. Wodehouse, whose comedic novels of British life among the "smart set" provide an exquisite counterpoint to the difficulties of Nell's own life.

This is a novel that shows us just how extraordinary an ordinary life really is. Nell lives through two wars, the Great Depression, and amazing technological change. She loses many of the people she loves, but she does not lose her capacity to love. She remains a warm, steadfast, caring character who will stay with the reader for a long time.

DISCUSSION/REFLECTION STRATEGIES

- Nell often refers to herself as "escaping" through literature, especially when she refers to reading Wodehouse. Is Nell's relationship with her novels a positive one? She certainly thinks so, but could there be another reading of the relationship to books when it comes to "escape"?

- This is a good time to think about your own relationship to novels. What books do you turn to in times of trouble, and why? Have you ever worried that you were escaping too far into the world of a particular book(s)? How can we know if what brings us comfort actually is a healing balm or a crutch that keeps us dependent?

Did You Know...?

Bibliotherapy is the practice of reading particular texts in order to treat ailments or overcome obstacles in one's life. It has a long history—even ancient Greek sages recommended bracing texts to people looking to grapple with the problems of existence—and modern brain studies show that fiction reading strengthens people's ability to experience empathy. To find out more, look for Ceridwen Dovey's article "Can Reading Make You Happier?" at NewYorker.com.

Also look for *The Novel Cure: From Abandonment to Zestlessness: 751 Books to Cure What Ails You,* by Ella Berthoud and Susan Elderkin. One of the ailments listed is "feeling overwhelmed by the number of books in the world."

EXTRA CREDIT

Fans of the novel might be interested in other books by Faith Sullivan that also take place in Harvester, Minnesota. *The Cape Ann, The Empress of One,* and *Gardenias* feature many of the characters from *Good Night, Mr. Wodehouse.*

READING LOLITA IN TEHRAN: A MEMOIR IN BOOKS

Azar Nafisi

ℒ

After she resigns from an academic teaching position in Tehran, Azar Nafisi invites seven of her brightest students to continue meeting with her every Thursday morning to read and discuss great literature together in the privacy of her home. It's not only privacy her home provides: it's also secrecy. Works of Western literature have been forbidden by the fundamentalist Islamic government, and Nafisi and her students put themselves in great danger by insisting, albeit quietly, on their right to read. Their discussions of *The Great Gatsby*, *Daisy Miller*, *Pride and Prejudice*, and of course *Lolita* are wide-ranging, moving easily from the world of the novel to the often oppressive and frightening world around them in Tehran, from their personal lives to the history of the Islamic Republic.

Through their conversations about these classic works of Western literature, Nafisi and her students get to know each other, and it is as much through their relationships with each other as through their relationships with the literature that they grow and change. This is a story about books and reading, yes, but even more, it is a story about reading in a particular place with particular people and how books and conversations about books can help us make sense of our lives.

DISCUSSION/REFLECTION STRATEGIES

- Although all of the books Nafisi reads with her group of students lead to significant reading experiences, Nabokov's novel *Lolita* becomes their touchstone reading experience. What are your own touchstone books, and which books have you returned to more than once in your life?

- Have you ever had an experience where the place or circumstances under which you're reading significantly impact your reading experience?

EXTRA CREDIT

Why not read books recommended by Nafisi herself? She includes a "Suggested Reading" list at the back of *Reading Lolita in Tehran*. Of course, the books she and her students read and discuss are here, but she also includes books that help explain Iran, such as Marjane Satrapi's marvelous graphic novel, *Persepolis*, as well as some favorite contemporary novels, such as Carol Shields's *Stone Diaries*, and Muriel Sparks's *Loitering with Intent*.

THE WORLD BETWEEN TWO COVERS: READING THE GLOBE

Ann Morgan

Fresh from a yearlong project concentrating on women writers and reflecting on her life at her popular blog, *A Year of Reading Women*, Ann Morgan embarks on a new adventure *cum* obsession: reading one work in English or translation from every country in the world. She creates a new blog, *A Year of Reading the World*, asks for recommendations, and begins reading and reviewing her way around the world in translated literature.

Only it isn't quite so easy as that. Even figuring out how many books she would read is fraught with difficulties: there is no universally accepted list of the nations of the world, and in fact, Morgan's plan changes halfway into her year of reading as she learns more about the politically charged situations that may lead to certain states being considered nations and others being denied nationhood.

The World Between Two Covers explores these and many other problems of trying to read globally, including cultural bias, censorship, the politics of publication, and the limitations of translation. This erudite yet readable study asks how we can approach global literature productively given all our disadvantages reading in different cultures.

DISCUSSION/REFLECTION STRATEGIES

- Morgan's reading-the-world project begins with a comment left on her blog by an Australian reader who recommends she read Tim Winton's *Cloudstreet*. This persistent blog reader's comments eventually lead Morgan to decide that her own reading life is "stunted and anemic" and in need of "corrective treatment." Are you satisfied with the variety and diversity of your own reading life? What correctives would you prescribe for yourself?

- Where would you start your own reading-around-the-world adventure? What countries, territories, geographical locations intrigue you the most? Lots of times, when traveling to a new country, people read a book from that country. If you've done this, how has it deepened your experience of travel?

EXTRA CREDIT

Morgan continues to advocate for world literature at her blog, *A Year of Reading the World*, where you can find enough reading recommendations for a lifetime of international reading. Morgan also has a popular TED Talk about her reading project, "My Year of Reading a Book from Every Country in the World."

November

COMFORT FOOD, COMFORT READING

- *The Light of the World: A Memoir* by Elizabeth Alexander
- *Life from Scratch: A Memoir of Food, Family, and Forgiveness* by Sasha Martin
- *Stir: My Broken Brain and the Meals That Brought Me Home* by Jessica Fechtor
- *Relish: My Life in the Kitchen* by Lucy Knisley
- *Yes, Chef: A Memoir* by Marcus Samuelsson

The interconnections among love, security, and food are present all year, but perhaps never so apparent as in November, when winter begins to set in and the holiday season beckons. The weather keeps us inside, the summer's harvest is celebrated, we settle in for the long winter ahead, making plans to see—and most certainly to eat with—family and friends. We'll be doing a lot of reading too…

THE LIGHT OF THE WORLD: A MEMOIR

Elizabeth Alexander

For fifteen years, poet and playwright Elizabeth Alexander had been happily married to her husband, chef and artist Ficre Ghebreyesus, when he unexpectedly died of heart failure caused by a heart condition that had gone undetected and undiagnosed. *The Light of the World* is her beautifully written memoir of their life together and her journey through grief after her husband's death. Many of Alexander's happiest memories of her husband are connected to the foods they prepared and ate together. Ghebreyesus was a joyful man with a huge appetite for the world. Alexander's warm prose captures that larger-than-life personality on the page and allows the reader to feel a real sense of loss when Ghebreyesus dies. By including some of their favorite recipes, she invites her readers to a special understanding of her and her husband's lives together.

The second half of the book is a meditation on mourning, especially in the absence of religious rituals. The reader suspects that writing this book is Alexander's most important act in the work of grieving. Although the book is deeply personal, its insights into love and loss have universal appeal.

DISCUSSION/REFLECTION STRATEGIES

- Food as nourishment, celebration, and an expression of love and family is a vital element of Alexander's marriage. After Ghebreyesus's death, Alexander cooks and serves delicious food as a ritual of remembrance and celebration of their life together. How is food part of your family's rituals and celebrations?

- Which of your go-to recipes are as much about a favorite dish as about remembering a loved one or special meal in your past?

Did You Know...?

In 2009, Alexander was selected to read a poem at President Obama's inauguration. She read a poem she wrote specially for the occasion called "Praise Song for the Day." You can see her perform the poem at the inauguration on YouTube. If you're interested in reading Alexander's poetry, we recommend *Crave Radiance: New and Selected Poems 1990–2010*, which includes her inauguration poem.

EXTRA CREDIT

Sometimes people complain that memoirs about loss are self-indulgent and a symptom of a culture that overshares. Other times, people argue that in the absence of uniform rituals and religious observance, we need to learn about grief through other people's experiences. Memoirs about grief that we recommend are:

- *A Grief Observed* by C. S. Lewis
- *The Year of Magical Thinking* by Joan Didion
- *Giving Up the Ghost: A Memoir* by Hilary Mantel
- *The Long Goodbye* by Meghan O'Rourke
- *Love Is a Mixtape: Life and Loss One Song at a Time* by Rob Sheffield

LIFE FROM SCRATCH: A MEMOIR OF FOOD, FAMILY, AND FORGIVENESS

Sasha Martin

Sasha Martin's early life was rough. Despite her mother's dexterity with a needle and thread and creativity with meals, the family was known to Boston's Department of Social Services and was frequently monitored. Sasha and her brother were even removed from their home and placed in foster care. Her beloved brother committed suicide, but despite her pain and the chaos of her life, Sasha graduates from Wesleyan University and becomes an MFK Fisher Scholar at the Culinary Institute of America.

This book, which started life as a "stunt memoir" (see facing page), is much, much more. Martin begins by setting herself a project in which she cooks a meal from every country in the world over the course of four years. She hopes to expand her family's food horizons and learn about the world in the process. What she does not expect, and what the reader is most grateful for, is what Martin learns about herself, her family, and the role of food in the deepening of relationships. Martin's life is laid bare in this memoir, but in a way that is ultimately affirming and one that readers, no matter what their own life is like, can relate to.

DISCUSSION/REFLECTION STRATEGIES

- Think about how the food of Martin's childhood impacts the choices she has made since growing up and making her way in the world. How does she use food as a way of reconnecting with her mother? How is food connected to creating the safe family life she was denied as a child?

- Martin makes the distinction between material poverty and spiritual poverty. Her family did not have much in the way of material goods, but was there a "poverty of the spirit" in her home?

- What food habits did you learn from your family? As an adult, what have you rejected...or at least not continued?

Did You Know...?

A **stunt memoir** is a book chronicling a particular challenge the author undertakes for a period of time. As in everything else, quality varies. "Okay, you're wearing only green clothes for a year; why am I reading this?" Other times, as with Martin's book, the so-called stunt becomes a framework by which the author discovers deeper insights into their lives and the lives of us all. Here are five of our favorite stunt memoirs:

- *The Happiness Project* by Gretchen Rubin
- *Nickel and Dimed: On (Not) Getting By in America* by Barbara Ehrenreich
- *Not Buying It: My Year without Shopping* by Judith Levine
- *Animal, Vegetable, Miracle: A Year of Food Life* by Barbara Kingsolver
- *The Winter of Our Disconnect* by Susan Maushart

EXTRA CREDIT

Some psychologists argue that food and eating mediate important aspects of relationships between mothers and daughters. Sometimes this is positive—as when mothers teach daughters food preparation skills and pass on family traditions. But food and eating can also become the destructive battleground on which displays of power are exercised or resisted. For insight into these issues, we recommend Kim Chernin's *The Hungry Self: Women, Eating, and Identity* and *The Obsession: Reflections on the Tyranny of Slenderness*.

Jessica Fechtor

Jessica Fechtor is twenty-eight, a graduate student at Harvard, married to the man of her dreams. She and her husband are about to start trying for a baby. They have their future mapped out, and everything is going their way—until Fechtor collapses from a brain hemorrhage, and life is never the same again. Fechtor eventually loses the sight in one eye, loses her sense of smell, and suffers from a life-threatening infection. Throughout all this, she remains focused on food. She asks visiting family and friends to describe the meals they have eaten, and she remembers cooking with her mother, her stepmother, and her grandmother. She conscientiously invokes her memories of food to have something besides her pain to occupy her.

This memoir, painful to read at times, is the story of how food nourishes our souls in addition to our bodies. Fechtor's long road to recovery consists of taking small steps to get back in the kitchen and back to her life.

DISCUSSION/REFLECTION STRATEGIES

- One of her doctors asks Fechtor why she thinks this brain hemorrhage happened to her. What do you think of her answer? What about her annoyance when people tell her that "everything happens for a reason"? What do you think when people tell you everything happened for a reason?

- Does reading about Fechtor's loss of her senses make you appreciate your own more? What is the meal you would miss the taste of most? Or the smell you take for granted?

- Does the inclusion of recipes at the end of chapters give the reader a much-needed break from the intensity of Fechtor's medical issues, or do you think it interrupts the flow of the story?

EXTRA CREDIT

Have a look at Fechtor's blog, *Sweet Amandine*. In the entry for June 11, 2015, she offers to speak with book clubs via Skype. What a great idea! Email her through the blog, have a few dates when your group is meeting and see if it works out. Make sure your group prepares some of Jessica's recipes for the occasion.

Do you read any food blogs? Do you have any favorites to share with others? If you haven't delved into the world of food obsessives online, then you are in for a treat. In addition to *Sweet Amandine*, have a look at *Smitten Kitchen,* where Deb Perelman produces fantastic treats from a tiny New York City kitchen. *Chocolate and Zucchini* is a brilliant site by Clotilde Desoulier, a French woman writing in English. David Lebovitz is an American chef living in Paris who writes cookbooks and focuses on chocolates and desserts at DavidLebovitz.com.

RELISH

Lucy Knisley

Lucy Knisley's graphic novel memoir offers a delightful trip down food memory lane. Like many foodies, Knisley finds she has "taste-memories": the flavors of certain foods trigger memories of long-forgotten events and experiences. Raised by a mother who loved to cook and made a career for herself as a caterer and a father who loved to eat, Lucy grows up surrounded by people who live to eat. As a child she's a fearless eater, downing oysters and even straight shots of vinegar as she makes vinaigrette with her father. Such foods would be exotic to most children, but for Lucy, the processed convenience foods most of us take for granted are exotic, even illicit. Junk food becomes a form of rebellion in her adolescence: nothing, it turns out, upsets her parents more than a hamburger and French fries from McDonald's. There is a place for every kind of food in Knisley's world, even bad food when it's lovingly prepared and shared with friends. *Relish* is a warm-hearted memoir about all the kinds of sustenance we can receive from food— comfort, pleasure, connection with family and friends, identity, culture. "When we eat, we take in more than just sustenance," she reminds us.

Each chapter ends with an illustrated recipe that readers will certainly want to try for themselves. We recommend brewing yourself a cup of Knisley's Spiced Tea and settling down to read the rest of the book. Be sure to spend some time with the afterword, a photo album with some of the family photos Knisley consulted to research her book.

DISCUSSION/REFLECTION STRATEGIES

- *Relish* is about food, but it's also about growing up and the key experiences and memories that help us transition from childhood to adulthood. What foods do you remember from your childhood, and why are they so vivid in your mind?

- Knisley's parents have strong opinions about food—such strong opinions, in fact, that we could even consider them food rules. What are your family's spoken and unspoken rules about food, and where do you think they came from?
- Are there any favorite childhood dishes that show up regularly on your dinner table?

Did You Know...?

Lucy Knisley has mined her life for material in five graphic novel memoirs that she wrote and illustrated in her twenties! *French Milk* is a travelogue of a journey she and her mother took to France to celebrate their birthdays. *An Age of License* recounts her adventures on a book tour in Europe as she explores with questions of identity and purpose. *Displacement: A Travelogue* is not nearly so lighthearted as her other books: in this travelogue, she grapples with aging and loss as she accompanies her elderly, failing grandparents on a cruise. Finally, *Something New: Tales from a Makeshift Bride* chronicles her engagement and adventures in wedding planning.

EXTRA CREDIT

Lucy Knisley maintains a Tumblr at LucyKnisley
.tumblr.com, where she posts drawings from her
sketchbook, news about publications and author
events, and comics. You can also find her twenty-
minute video, "Life Is the Story," which describes how
she and others create autobiographical travelogues.

YES, CHEF: A MEMOIR

Marcus Samuelsson

If you've eaten at one of Samuelsson's New York restaurants, read his cookbooks, or seen him on TV shows *Top Chef Masters* or *Chopped*, you'll easily believe he knows his food. After you read *Yes, Chef*, written with the assistance of Veronica Chambers, you will also know that he can really write. *Yes, Chef* is an evocative memoir of Samuelsson's life in and around the kitchen. To understand how Samuelsson cooks, the unique fusion of many cultures and cuisines, it's necessary to understand his life.

He was born in Ethiopia and adopted by a Swedish couple when he was just a toddler. Ethiopian cooking, which he learned as an adult, and Swedish cooking, which he learned from his grandmother and from cooking school in Sweden, are two of his primary influences. *Yes, Chef* blends memories of Samuelsson's childhood growing up in Sweden with stories from the famous kitchens where he has worked, as well as tales from his extensive travels around the world. Most of all, *Yes, Chef* reveals the extraordinary drive and talent it takes to become one of the world's most recognized and honored chefs.

DISCUSSION/REFLECTION STRATEGIES

- Which storyline is most engaging to you in *Yes, Chef*: Samuelsson's remembrances of childhood to manhood or his quest to become a master chef? What parts of each resonate particularly strongly?
- Samuelsson's determination to be the best reveals his powerful ambition and work ethic. In your opinion, what are the plusses and minuses of a life lived with this kind of drive? Is ambition always an intrinsic part of a strong work ethic?

Did You Know...?

Have you heard of the **Slow Food Movement**? Founded in 1986 in Italy, the Slow Food Movement dedicates itself to preserving and reviving regional cuisines and eating habits. The movement argues that "fast food" is more than just bad food cheaply priced. It is gastronomically and nutritionally poor; it forces local food purveyors out of business, thereby hurting local economies; and it contributes to the breakdown of the family and society by undermining the practice of preparing food and eating together. The Slow Food Movement consists of *convivia,* or clubs, sharing meals and cooking techniques, educating one another about local farming practices, and organizing against the incursion of fast-food outlets in historic regions. Find out more at slowfood.com.

⁝ EXTRA CREDIT ⁝

If you enjoy cooking, try cooking some recipes from one of Marcus Samuelsson's cookbooks. *Aquavit and the New Scandinavian Cuisine*, his first cookbook, shares recipes and techniques he used to modernize Scandinavian cooking at the famed New York restaurant, Aquavit, where he was executive chef. *The Soul of a New Cuisine* represents Samuelsson's brand of fusion at its best: for this book, he traveled through Africa to find and modernize traditional African recipes. *New American Table* shares his take on modern American cuisine. Finally, *Off Duty: The Recipes I Cook at Home* shares recipes Samuelsson cooks for his family and friends.

December

HEARTWARMING CLASSICS

- *A Tree Grows in Brooklyn* by Betty Smith
- *Little Women* by Louisa May Alcott
- *Anne of Green Gables* by L. M. Montgomery
- *The 100* Best African American Poems* edited by Nikki Giovanni
- *A Christmas Carol* by Charles Dickens and Dono Sanchez Almara

Most of these books you have already read. Some of them you may have read repeatedly, even obsessively. Maybe you *were* Jo March; maybe you wanted to be Anne Shirley. We hope you will take the time at this hectic holiday season to remind yourself of the gift of reading and rediscover the joy it has brought you by renewing your acquaintance with this month's classic stories and poems.

A TREE GROWS IN BROOKLYN

Betty Smith

Francie Nolan lives in Brooklyn during the early years of the twentieth century. We are introduced to Francie when she is eleven years old, and we say good-bye to her as she leaves for college. Through Francie we meet her father, the charming but alcoholic Johnny Nolan, and her mother, Katie Nolan, still young and beautiful but burdened with trying to keep the family fed and housed. Francie's younger brother, Neeley, shares Francie's adventures and her dreams of a more stable life.

Francie is our guide to the borough, showing us its vitality, its energy, the joys and sorrows that afflict its residents. Early twentieth-century Brooklyn was home to an astonishing mixture of recent immigrants living in close proximity: we meet Chinese tea merchants, Jewish peddlers, Irish bartenders, and German laborers. Smith's gaze never flinches from the hard reality of these people's lives. She chronicles domestic violence, alcoholism, unemployment, and the grinding degradation of poverty, but she also reveals to us the strength of these people and demands that we acknowledge the dignity inherent in their lives.

DISCUSSION/REFLECTION STRATEGIES

- Ethnic slurs for different people are part of the everyday language of the characters and might shock the modern reader. Does this affect how you understand the characters and their lives, or your ability to empathize with the characters?

- What circumstances of the characters' lives encourage ethnic divisiveness and name-calling? Consider the fact that within Brooklyn, the different ethnic enclaves are close to one another and interdependent: for example, the Irish characters shop at Jewish grocery stores and go to Chinese launderers. People may use crude stereotypes to describe one another, but they are at least interacting with one another daily.

- Critics note that Brooklyn is the real protagonist of the novel rather than Francie. What other places—in real life or in fiction—stand out for you as locations worthy of "starring roles" in novels?

EXTRA CREDIT

When you visit Brooklyn today, you have to search a bit to find the remnants of the borough that Betty Smith describes. Unlike for most of its history, it is now a sought-after place to live with hip coffee shops and rising home prices. The following five books each describe different facets of the borough.

- *My Korean Deli: Risking It All for a Convenience Store* by Ben Ryder Howe
- *Daddy Was a Number Runner* by Louise Meriwether
- *Brown Girl, Brownstones* by Paule Marshall
- *When I Was Puerto Rican* by Esmeralda Santiago
- *The Chosen* by Chaim Potok

LITTLE WOMEN

Louisa May Alcott

ℓ

Louisa May Alcott's classic tale of the poor but happy March family made her a celebrity upon its publication in 1868 and has been adored by generations of young—and not-so-young—readers ever since. Part I follows the March sisters and their mother through the privations of the Civil War when their father is away fighting. Loosely modeled after *Pilgrim's Progress*, *Little Women*'s first part is a moral tale of the trials that build character and discipline in Christians. But it is also a funny and vividly rendered "domestic drama" of four sisters struggling to grow up. Part II, originally published separately as *Good Wives*, opens three years later and follows the March sisters as they marry and establish families of their own. For many of us, reading *Little Women* as adults is rereading, a chance to revisit ourselves as young readers, a chance to remember and interrogate the understanding and expectations we brought to an earlier reading life. If you are reading the novel for the first time, prepare to be transported to mid-nineteenth-century Massachusetts and meet characters who will become friends for life.

DISCUSSION/REFLECTION STRATEGIES

- Scholar Ann Douglas claims, "What plot there is in *Little Women* runs contrary to Jo's wishes." What are Jo's wishes, and why do her desires resonate so strongly with the reader?

- Many readers who fall in love with this novel as young women exclaim that they were Jo March. What is so appealing about her character? Does anyone in your reading group identify more with another character?

- Alcott has been criticized by literary scholars for writing didactic novels. Her publisher urged her to provide, in a sense, a conduct manual for young girls. What model for conduct does *Little Women* inculcate in its readers?

- Why is this novel still so popular when standards for behavior, gender roles, and morality are different today?

Did You Know...?

Little Women is a **Bildungsroman**, a German term meaning a novel of formation. The *Bildungsroman* typically traces the development—emotional, intellectual, and social—of its protagonist as he or she grows up and tries to find a place in society. The quest plot often provides the structure for the *Bildungsroman*.

A **Künstlerroman** is a special kind of *Bildungsroman*: a novel focusing on the growth of an artist. James Joyce's *Portrait of the Artist as a Young Man* is a classic example. To what extent does *Little Women* offer a female version of the *Künstlerroman*?

ANNE OF GREEN GABLES

L. M. Montgomery

Poor Anne! She has spent her first eleven years living in orphanages, and now that she has finally been adopted, she finds it has all been a mistake. The older couple, who are brother and sister, wanted to adopt a boy to help with the farm work. But they get Anne instead, so they will have to send her back—which is too bad for Anne, who has already fallen in love with Prince Edward Island and the house of Green Gables. Decency, kindness, and Anne's enthusiasm win the day, and Anne is allowed to stay on.

Anne's adventures at Green Gables have delighted generations of readers around the world since 1908. Anne always has the best of intentions, but nothing ever goes according to plan. Like the time she prepares the pudding incorrectly and a mouse gets in and drowns. Or the time she inadvertently gets her best friend drunk. Still, Anne's enthusiasm for life and for anything that "gives scope to the imagination" makes her an endearing heroine and a lifelong friend for the reader.

DISCUSSION/REFLECTION STRATEGIES

- Quick! How many redheaded heroines of children's books can you think of? Besides Anne, we have Pippi Longstocking and…? Why are there so many, and what do these characters have in common other than their hair color?

- Why do you think Anne's appeal has been universal and long-lasting? Did you have any "Anne moments" in your childhood?

Did You Know...?

Anne of Green Gables is hugely popular in Japan. In 1939, a children's literature translator, Hanako Muraoka, was given a copy of the novel. She spent the war years working on a translation and the result was *Akage no An*, or *Red-Haired Anne*, published in 1952. The book has been popular in Japan ever since. Since then, there has been an *anime* adaptation in 1979, still regularly televised, and a Japanese-language musical adaptation. There was even, for a while, an Anne-inspired theme park in Japan, and abroad Japanese visitors to Prince Edward Island are many. *Hanako to Anne* is a Japanese television dramatic series, which debuted in 2014, about the life of the Japanese translator. Look for Terry Dawes's article "Why *Anne of Green Gables* Is Big in Japan" for more information.

EXTRA CREDIT

Check out Beulah Devaney's article "Where Have All the Red-Headed Heroines Gone?" on ForBooksSake.net. If you want to know more, look for *Red: A History of the Redhead* by Jacky Colliss Harvey.

THE 100* BEST
AFRICAN AMERICAN POEMS

Edited by Nikki Giovanni

This spirited collection of great poems by African American poets needs an asterisk and a footnote in the title because, as editor Nikki Giovanni explains in her introduction, "I cheated...The idea of *this* and no more would simply not work for me. I needed *these* plus *those*." Luckily, Giovanni's inability to limit herself to just one hundred poems works out well for her readers, who are treated to extra poems by Langston Hughes, Gwendolyn Brooks, and more. Extra poems aren't the only bonus in this collection:

the book was also published with a CD of performances of thirty-six of the poems, some read by the poets themselves, some by other poets, actors, and friends of Giovanni. These poems really come to life when they're performed by exceptional readers: you may be surprised at how your understanding and appreciation of a poem deepen when you hear it performed.

Many of the classic poems and poets you'd expect to find in a book of the hundred best African American poems are here: Langston Hughes's "Theme for English B"; Robert Hayden's "Those Winter Sundays"; Gwendolyn Brooks's "We Real Cool." But Giovanni's interests and tastes are wide-ranging, and even devoted readers of poetry will find new works and new authors to celebrate and all types of poetry to explore: political poems, celebrations, dirges, praise poems, polemics.

DISCUSSION/REFLECTION STRATEGIES

- Ask yourself these questions as you read a poem:
  - What does the poem seem to be about? What is the poet saying?
  - Look for images, striking phrases, word choice, and word patterns. What pictures form in your mind as you're reading? What lines stand out? Do these pictures or lines relate to the overall meaning?
  - What impact do the poet's choices about form have on your experience of the poem? Consider both how the poem looks to the eye (the line breaks, the division into stanzas) and how it rings in the ear (the rhyme scheme, if any, and the meter). Would other choices have worked as well?
  - How does the title relate to the poem?

EXTRA CREDIT

If you enjoy listening to performances of poetry, check out *Poetry Speaks Expanded: Hear Poets Read from Their Own Work from Tennyson to Plath* and *Hip Hop Speaks to Children: A Celebration of Poetry with a Beat*. Both collections come with CDs.

A CHRISTMAS CAROL

Charles Dickens
and Dono Sanchez Almara

You may know the story. Bob Cratchit works long hours as a clerk for Mr. Ebenezer Scrooge, trying to keep his family from succumbing to poverty in Victorian England.

We can safely say that the wealthy Mr. Scrooge is a not very pleasant man. He hates Christmas, responding to most utterances of the word "Christmas" with "Humbug." Although he lives alone, he spurns a dinner invitation on Christmas from his nephew. And while he does allow Bob Cratchit to have the day off he complains bitterly about it.

On Christmas Eve, Scrooge has strange visitors. The first is his long-dead business partner, Jacob Marley, who warns him against his miserly ways, and his appearance is followed by the Ghost of Christmas Past, the Ghost of Christmas Present, and the Ghost of Christmas Yet to Come.

Dono Sanchez Almara's graphic-novel version of *A Christmas Carol* is vibrant and evocative, and although it is an abridged version of the novel, it does not sacrifice the essential messages of the original text.

DISCUSSION/REFLECTION STRATEGIES

- *A Christmas Carol* has not been out of print since it was published in 1843. There have been multiple print versions, movie adaptations, theater productions, and graphic novels. Nearly every situation comedy one can think of has a holiday episode that draws directly from *A Christmas Carol*. Why is this story so popular, and why has it become such an entrenched part of our annual celebrations?

- In any version of the story, it is Scrooge who is always the central figure. Did Dickens mean for the reader to identify with Scrooge? Are we all Scrooges in some way or another?

 **Have You Seen the Movie?**

There are many film adaptations of *A Christmas Carol*. Try one or more of the following and show excerpts at your book group meeting. Who makes the best Scrooge?

- *Scrooge*, directed by Brian Desmond Hunt, 1951, and starring Alastair Sim in the title role. This version is traditional, and faithful to the text.

- *Scrooged*, directed by Richard Donner, 1988. In this updating of the story, Bill Murray stars as a ruthless television network executive with no apparent sense of humanity at all.

- *The Muppet Christmas Carol*, directed by Brian Henson, 1992. This version featuring Michael Caine as Scrooge is kid friendly, and mixes live actors with puppets.

- *A Christmas Carol*, directed by Robert Zemeckis, 2009. This animated version of the classic features voices by Jim Carrey, Gary Oldman, and Colin Firth.

✃ BOOK GROUPS ✄

FAQs for Book Group Beginners

How do I find a book group to join?

- Ask at your local library. If they don't run one themselves, they will know who is running one. Get to know your librarian.

- Ask your local bookseller. Bookstores run their own groups sometimes, but if they don't, they are likely to know people in the community who do.

- Even in the digital age, you can get a lot of information from bulletin boards in community centers.

- Local places of worship are great places to find people and reading groups.

- Check online—Google "book group" and your town and see what comes up!

I want to start my own group. How do I find people to join?

- Word of mouth is your best friend here. Tell friends, neighbors, and coworkers.

- Post notices at your local library and bookstore.

- Use an existing group as a springboard for a reading group. For example, if you belong to a craft club, see if some of the members would like to form a book club.

- If you have children, ask the parents you meet at sports events or recitals if they're interested. You could even combine a reading group with another activity, like discussing books while waiting for the kids' soccer practice to finish.

- Go where the readers are. Public readings and lectures, library programs, author events, and adult education classes are great places to meet fellow book enthusiasts.

How many people should be in my book group?

At least eight and no more than twelve make for the perfect book group. Fewer than eight people and you all might be struggling for something to say. More than twelve and people tend to drift into side conversations. And with twelve people, if you're sharing hosting duties, then each member only hosts once per year.

Where should we meet?

- Members' homes. You can rotate or have it at the same place each time. We recommend rotating to spread out the burden of hosting.

- Coffee shop—Ask your friendly barista if you can meet there regularly. If they have enough room and a schedule of when you will be there, they will welcome you with open arms.
- Local library, house of worship, or bookshop.
- Weather permitting, what about meeting outside? Find a nearby park (bring a picnic!) or go on a hike (not too strenuous) and talk while getting some exercise.
- Museums frequently have meeting rooms for community use and/or lovely gardens and coffee shops. Combine your discussion group with a visit to the galleries.

What should you do at the first meeting?

If your group is new, try an ice-breaker exercise. Create a quiz with questions like:

- Who has hiked the Appalachian Trail?
- Who has lived in a foreign country?
- Who speaks more than one language?
- Who has four or more brothers and sisters?
- Who owns more than three pets?

To fill out the quiz, each member must walk around the room and find someone who meets the criterion in question. (Or ask each person to write down three books or three things that they would take with them if they had to be stranded on a desert island. Share the answers.)

Get down to business and discuss what types of books you'd like to read. Will your group have a theme (for example, women's literature, works of history, romance, science fiction)? Have suggestions ready for the next meeting's selection. Someone should also volunteer to collect names and contact information and have this available for everyone at the next meeting or send it to the members via email. Set a date and time for the next meeting and ask for a volunteer to bring snacks.

How do we find books to suggest to our group?

You've come to the right place: with sixty annotated selections and scores of additional suggestions, *A Year of Reading* should keep your reading club busy for some time. If you do run out before we come to write the third edition, here are some other options:

- Make a commitment to read book reviews. The *New York Times Book Review* is an important source of information and criticism about what's out there and what is worth reading. It's available via the Sunday paper, is sold separately, and is available online.

- When we can find them, we're fond of quirky catalogs like *Bas Bleu*.

- Blogs are huge for finding options to read. Elisabeth Ellington blogs at *The Dirigible Plum*. Elisabeth is the coauthor of this book and a prolific reader and writer. Visit her blog to find out what's going on in the world of young adult fiction and graphic novels. The website Reviewing the Evidence is a great resource for crime fiction.

- Join Goodreads for an online community of book lovers.

How do we choose which books to read?

There a few different ways of doing this:

- Schedule a "selection meeting" for twice a year. Each member brings three books he or she thinks would work for the group. This gives your group a substantial pool from which to choose. Look at the selections; vote on what to read.

- Spend fifteen minutes at the beginning or ending of the monthly meeting determining what to read for the next month. Don't let the conversation get carried away: it's possible to spend hours talking over options!

- Give each member the power to assign a book for any given month.

Experiment with different styles until you discover what works for you.

Am I going to have to cook for all these people?

Many book groups meet at members' homes over dinner. But this needn't be too much trouble. The host provides a simple main course like soup or pasta, and other members can bring a salad or dessert. If you keep the meal simple and split up the responsibility, no one person will be overburdened. Of course, you may decide just to have snacks or desserts. Remember that food is secondary to conversation: don't get competitive with food preparation or feel that you have to serve food that complements the book (though that can be fun).

What guidelines does our group need?

A book group is, first and foremost, a community of book lovers, and all members must feel valued and respected for the community to thrive. So how do you resolve minor irritations, or deal with those reluctant to take turns, contribute to the discussion, or be the host? With great tact and gentle remonstrance, of course.

Who is responsible for speaking up? The best troubleshooting tip is to spend time with your group brainstorming potential problems, along with solutions with which the whole group can agree. This can save worry, stress, and help avoid hurt feelings. When emotions are high, it is difficult to be detached and objective.

One surefire way to deal with the most common problems is to be prepared with our Five Key Comments:

- *"That is interesting. I'd like to hear what everyone else has to say."* You say this to people who habitually go on a bit too much about their own concerns.

- *"I am interested in the average annual rainfall in Bolivia, but I would really like to continue talking about the book—I especially want to address question three from* A Year of Reading.*"* Okay, you had been discussing expeditions to the Antarctic because that is what your selection is about, but somehow the discussion has meandered into Bolivian climate patterns. Don't complain, just remind everyone to get back to the book.

- *"Do you all think we need to start being more formal about scheduling our hosting and food providing? I could be wrong, but it seems like the same people are always volunteering."* No need to mention names. Just bring the issue up to the group. The nonvolunteers usually get the message.

- *"Would you like to ride with my carpool next month? I think the meetings go better when we all arrive on time."* Say this to the habitually late person.

- *"Tell us about one of your favorite books. What do you like about it?"* This is for the person who hates every book your group reads. Nonstop negativity is easy to deliver, but tough to listen to month after month. Turn the tables. Get them to explain what they like and why. Ask them to recommend a book for the next meeting.

⌘ Twenty-One Ways ⌘ to Build a Better Book Group

1. **Stay in touch in between meetings.** Send out reminders of upcoming meetings: where it is, what the book is, and who is bringing the cake. Share book recommendations, continue the discussion from the last meeting, announce members' news (birthdays, babies, etc.). You can do this via a Facebook page or through a group blog.

2. **Keep a record of what your group reads.** Sure, you think you'll never forget, but keep a record of your reading. It's helpful when you are planning for the next year, and it introduces your shared literary history to prospective new members.

3. **Establish a policy for admitting new members.** It stands to reason that when you lose members—as you inevitably will to life circumstances—you may want to add new people. Fresh members can breathe new life into a group through the different experience, ideas, and reading interests they bring. **Do** discuss how many members you think are optimal for your group. Think carefully about how well you know a person and what they can bring to the group. **Don't** extend membership to the group without checking with your book club first.

4. **Your group needs a guest policy.** Your book group is terrific. Your selections are strong, the people are enthusiastic, and conversation flows. Now your non–book group friends want to get involved. They want to visit your book group. In fact, everyone has a friend who wants to visit the group. Should friends be allowed to visit? What happens to the sense of trust your book group shares if strange people keep showing up?

   Here are some dos and don'ts for inviting guests:

   > **Do** ask your group ahead of time if they would mind if you brought someone.

   > **Don't** just show up with a surprise guest—it's rude.

Do introduce your friend to everyone.

Do have your friend read the book selection.

Do encourage guests to participate.

Don't change your format too much to accommodate the guest.

Best of all, **do** designate one month as a guest month where members can all bring a friend.

5. **Deal with absenteeism.** It happens to all of us: a busy month when we don't have time to read the book or when other commitments intervene on our reading group night. But when this happens month after month with the same people, or when so few members show up that discussion fails, absenteeism has become a problem in the group. The best way to solve it is to institute policies early on. We know some groups that have instituted a policy of three-strikes-and-you're-out: if any member misses three meetings in a row, she is asked to leave the group. There are also gentler ways of roping in absentees. When a member misses a meeting, why not call or send an email, bringing him up to date on what you've read and what's on the schedule for next month.

6. **Be flexible about expectations of friendship.** Wouldn't it be wonderful if everyone in your book group adored one another and formed a tightly knit community whose members were always there for one another? Sure it would, but this probably won't happen. You may become close to some people in your

group—seeing them outside of the book group and introducing your children to theirs. But this may not happen. Members may not have the time and the inclination to socialize outside of book group, and that is okay too. It's perfectly acceptable just to see these folks once a month and talk about books. Be careful, though, if you do become more socially involved with others in the group. You don't have to hide friendship, but don't form a "clique" within the group that might make others uncomfortable, e.g., no private jokes, no significant glances.

7. **Get to know your local library and bookshop**. Let them know what books you are planning on reading and ask them to get multiple copies. Start with the library and see if you can get some copies for borrowing. Also check secondhand bookshops and used books online to help keep costs down. Librarians and booksellers always know what is out there, and they are more than willing to share their knowledge. Tell them which books invoked great discussions from your group and find out from them what other groups are reading.

8. **Find creative ways to pass on your books when you're finished with them.** Some members will want to keep all the group's reading selections. Others, not so much. You can easily sell your used books online. But consider donating them to libraries, nursing homes, homeless shelters, and high schools.

9. **Improve discussions by having a group leader for each session.** The group leader can research information about the author's life before the meeting and share interesting passages from interviews and biographies. Group discussion improves a lot when one person goes to the trouble to organize talking points. Prepare a few questions or comments to spark discussion. Use the questions we provide, and note that a lot of contemporary books come with reading club questions at the back.

10. **Experiment with a theme.** Concentrating on a particular type of literature or time period allows you to branch out into related topics. For example, if you focus on African literature, you can listen to and discuss indigenous music, read up on visual artists, and study some relevant history. Reading all the works of a particular author allows you to chart the changes he or she makes over time: Which themes recur? How does the treatment of them change?

11. **Experiment with genre.** Changing the type of book you choose for one or two meetings per year is probably the easiest, most painless way to add oomph to your group. Suggest something new for the sake of challenge or change. If your group reads popular fiction, try a volume of poetry or a classic. If you read literary fiction, explore science fiction or a detective novel. Even if you don't think much of the title or genre your group selects, you can still initiate a lively discussion about the merits

of generic divisions and the standards for inclusion in a particular genre.

12. **Go beyond "I liked it."** If your group finds it hard to move beyond a discussion of whether or not you liked the book, try some of these strategies:

> **Do** prepare some comments or questions.
>
> **Don't** do homework on the book—just make a few notes as you're reading.
>
> **Don't** dismiss issues you find puzzling or you don't understand. Talk about them.
>
> **Do** think about characters. Move beyond whether or not you liked a particular character by discussing her motivation for behaving as she did, looking at other characters' responses to this character, or thinking about why the author might want to create this character.
>
> **Do** think about setting and theme. Ask why the author wrote the story in this particular way. What other ways could the story be told?
>
> **Do** consider similar books or authors—or even films. If your group has trouble sustaining a discussion about one book, comparing and contrasting with another book or film should open up many avenues for discussion.

13. **Compare the book to the movie.** Read the book and then watch the film together. What's different about them? Has the

director remained faithful to the author's vision? Has the director changed details, but captured the essence of the book? Or has the film totally missed the point? Try to think of movies that are better than the books they are adapted from.

14. **Share a meal.** Groups often become closer when they start cooking together. Divide up the responsibilities, keep food choices simple, and everyone will be happy.

15. **Create your own book group rituals.** Hold a summer meeting outdoors, attend a local film festival yearly, exchange small gifts during the holiday.

16. **Build a greener book group.** Do some of the following: carpool, walk, or bike to meetings if possible. Surely a ten-person group doesn't need to take nine cars to a meeting. Use cloth napkins at meetings, and just throw them in the laundry basket after the meeting. And no, no one will mind if you haven't ironed them. Read a classic of the environmental movement like *Silent Spring* by Rachel Carson. Check your library for book group selections before heading to the bookstore. Make arrangements to share books with other members.

17. **What to do about sensitive topics?** Suppose the book you are reading deals with cancer, suicide, alcoholism, or child abuse? It's not unusual for someone in the group to have some

experience with the issue under discussion, and it is also not un-usual for that fact to emerge during discussion. Group members may respond to personal disclosure by feeling uncomfortable and trying to change the subject; however, a personal disclosure can open up discussion, taking it to a deeper level. How your group responds may depend upon how long you've been meet-ing, how close you are to one another, and the manner in which the disclosure has been raised. If someone volunteers personal information, listen, but do not try to "fix" the problem. If you are the person revealing the information, keep in mind that your book group probably wants the best for you, but may not know how to respond to your disclosure.

18. **Build in social time.** Book groups are social events, so build in social time at the beginning or end of your meeting. Long-lasting book groups endure because members create a support-ive, fun group environment. They look forward to seeing each other each month and finding out what the other members think about the book, but they're also eager to find out what's been happening since they last saw each other. They are no lon-ger acquaintances, but friends—even if they only see each other once a month for the book group meeting. How do you create a fun group? Get to know each other better. Find out where peo-ple work, who has partners or children, what people do in their spare time. Half an hour spent catching up is time well spent.

19. **Celebrate each other's personal milestones.** Have everyone sign a card for a birthday. Chip in for a gift and card to celebrate a new baby, a wedding, a new job.

20. **Form a spin-off group.** Pursue shared interests outside the setting of a reading group by forming a spin-off group. Form a film club or learn how to knit or sew together. Learning a language can be a great way to grow intellectually and to broaden your horizons. Call your local recreation department or university's continuing education program to sign up for classes.

❦ BOOKS MENTIONED ❧

Achebe, Chinua. *There Was a Country: A Memoir*. New York: Penguin, 2013.

Adams, Douglas. *The Hitchhiker's Guide to the Galaxy*. New York: Harmony Books, 1980.

Adichie, Chimamanda Ngozi. *Half of a Yellow Sun*. New York: Anchor, 2007.

———. *We Should All Be Feminists*. New York: Anchor, 2015.

Ahmed, Qanta A. *In the Land of Invisible Women: A Female Doctor's Journey in the Saudi Kingdom*. Naperville, IL: Sourcebooks, 2008.

Alcott, Louisa May. *Little Women*. Philadelphia, PA: Courage Books, 1995.

Alexander, Elizabeth. *Crave Radiance: New and Selected Poems 1990–2010*. Minneapolis, MN: Graywolf, 2012.

———. *The Light of the World: A Memoir*. New York: Grand Central, 2015.

Allende, Isabel. *The House of the Spirits*. New York: Atria, 2015.

Ansari, Aziz and Eric Klinenberg. *Modern Romance*. New York: Penguin, 2015.

Armstrong, Heather B. *It Sucked and Then I Cried: How I Had a Baby, a Breakdown, and a Much Needed Margarita*. New York: Simon Spotlight, 2009.

Austen, Jane. *Pride and Prejudice*. London: Penguin Classics, 2002.

Banks, Coleman. *The Essential Rumi*. New York: HarperOne, 2004.

———. *A Year with Rumi: Daily Reading*. New York: HarperOne, 2006.

Barry, Lynda. *What It Is*. Montreal: Drawn and Quarterly, 2008.

Berthoud, Ella and Susan Elderkin. *The Novel Cure: From Abandonment to Zestlessness: 751 Books to Cure What Ails You*. New York: Penguin, 2013.

Bissell, Tom. *Extra Lives: Why Video Games Matter*. New York: Pantheon, 2010.

Block, Francesca Lia. *Guarding the Moon: A Mother's First Year*. New York: Harper Collins, 2003.

Bolaño, Roberto. *The Savage Detectives*. New York: Pan Macmillan, 2015.

Booker, Sheri. *Nine Years Under: Coming of Age in an Inner-City Funeral Home*. New York: Gotham Books, 2013.

Boylan, Jennifer Finney. *She's Not There: A Life in Two Genders*. New York: Broadway Books, 2013.

———. *Stuck in the Middle with You: A Memoir of Parenting in Three Genders*. New York: Broadway Books, 2014.

Burrowes, Grace. *Tremaine's True Love*. Naperville, IL: Sourcebooks Casablanca, 2015.

Byrd, Ayana D. and Lori L. Tharps. *Hair Story: Untangling the Roots of Black Hair in America*. New York: St. Martin's Press, 2014.

Cameron, Julia. *The Artist's Way: A Spiritual Path to Higher Creativity*. New York: Jeremy B. Tarcher/Putnam, 2002.

Castranova, Edward. *Synthetic Worlds: The Business and Culture of Online Games*. Chicago: University of Chicago Press, 2006.

Cather, Willa. *My Ántonia*. Mineola, NY: Dover Publications, 1994.

Chast, Roz. *Can't We Talk about Something More Pleasant?* New York: Bloomsbury, 2014.

Chernin, Kim. *The Hungry Self: Women, Eating, and Identity*. New York: Times Books, 1985.

———. *The Obsession: Reflections on the Tyranny of Slenderness*. New York: Harper Perennial, 1994.

Coates, Ta-Nehisi. *The Beautiful Struggle: A Father, Two Sons, and an Unlikely Road to Manhood*. New York: Spiegel & Grau, 2009.

———. *Between the World and Me*. New York: Spiegel & Grau, 2015.

Colwin, Laurie. *Happy All the Time*. New York: Vintage Books, 2010.

Cunningham, Michael. *A Home at the End of the World*. New York: Farrar, Strauss & Giroux, 1990.

———. *The Hours*. New York: Picador, 1998.

Cusk, Rachel. *A Life's Work: On Becoming a Mother*. New York: Picador, 2001.

Daum, Meghan, ed. *Selfish, Shallow and Self-Absorbed: Sixteen Writers on the Decision Not to Have Kids*. New York: Picador, 2015.

Dawkins, Jane. *Letters from Pemberley: The First Year*. Naperville, IL: Sourcebooks, 2007.

Dessen, Sarah. *The Moon and More*. New York: Dutton Books, 2015.

Dev, Sonali. *The Bollywood Bride*. New York: Kensington Books, 2015.

Dickens, Charles and Dono Sanchez Almara. *A Christmas Carol: A Graphic Novel*. North Mankato, MN: Stone Arch, 2015.

Didion, Joan. *The Year of Magical Thinking*. New York: Harper Collins, 2009.

Diski, Jenny. *Skating to Antarctica*. London: Virago, 2005.

Doctorow, Cory and Jen Wang. *In Real Life*. New York: FirstSecond, 2014.

Eggers, Dave. *The Circle*. New York: Vintage, 2014.

Ehrenreich, Barbara. *Nickel and Dimed: On (Not) Getting By in America*. New York: Picador, 2011.

Ehrenreich, Barbara and Deirdre English. *Witches, Midwives, and Nurses: A History of Women Healers*. New York: Feminist Press, 2010.

Eisner, Will. *A Contract with God and Other Tenement Stories*. Princeton, WI: Kitchen Sink Press, 1985.

Erdrich, Louise. *The Painted Drum*. New York: Harper Perennial, 2005.

Fechtor, Jessica. *Stir: My Broken Brain and the Meals that Brought Me Home*. New York: Penguin Random House, 2015.

Gawande, Atul. *Being Mortal: Medicine and What Matters in the End*. New York: Metropolitan Books, 2014.

Gilbert, Daniel. *Stumbling on Happiness*. New York: Random House, 2006.

Gilbert, Elizabeth. *Big Magic: Creative Living beyond Fear*. New York: Riverhead Books, 2015.

Giovanni, Nikki, ed. *Hip Hop Speaks to Children: A Celebration of Poetry with a Beat*. Naperville, IL: Sourcebooks, 2008.

———, ed. *The 100 Best African American Poems*. Naperville, IL: Sourcebooks, 2010.

Guevara, Che. *The Motorcycle Diaries: Notes on a Latin American Journey*. North Melbourne, Australia: Ocean Press, 2003.

Gulledge, Laura Lee. *Page by Paige*. New York: Amulet Books, 2011.

Harding, Kate. *Asking for It: The Alarming Rise of Rape Culture—And What We Can Do about It*. Boston: De Capo Press, 2015.

Harjo, Joy. *Crazy Brave*. New York: W. W. Norton, 2012.

Harvey, Jacky Colliss. *Red: A History of the Redhead*. New York: Hachette, 2015.

Hassler, Alfred and Benton Resnick. *Martin Luther King and the Montgomery Story*. 1957. Marietta, GA: Top Shelf Productions, 2013.

Heyer, Georgette. *Venetia*. Naperville, IL: Sourcebooks Casablanca, 2011.

Holt, Hazel. *A Lot to Ask: A Life of Barbara Pym*. London: Bello Books, 2013.

Howard, Elizabeth Jane. *The Light Years (The Cazalet Chronicle)*. New York: Washington Square Press, 1995.

———. *Slipstream*. London: Pan Books, 2002.

Howe, Ben Ryder. *My Korean Deli: Risking It All for a Convenience Store*. New York: Henry Holt, 2010.

Jackson, Naomi A. *The Star Side of Bird Hill*. New York, Penguin, 2015.

Jacobs A. J. *Drop Dead Healthy: One Man's Humble Quest for Bodily Perfection*. New York: Simon & Schuster, 2012.

———. *The Know-It-All: One Man's Humble Quest to Become the Smartest Person in the World*. New York: Simon & Schuster, 2005.

James, P. D. *Death Comes to Pemberley*. New York: Alfred A. Knopf, 2011.

Jemisin, N. K. *The Fifth Season*. New York: Orbit, 2015.

Johnson, Alaya Dawn. *The Summer Prince*. New York: Arthur A. Levine Books, 2013.

Joyce, James. *A Portrait of the Artist as a Young Man*. New York: Penguin, 1993.

Kalman, Maira. *The Principles of Uncertainty*. New York: Penguin Press, 2007.

Kingsolver, Barbara. *Animal, Vegetable, Miracle: A Year of Food Life*. New York: Harper Perennial, 2007.

Kleon, Austin. *Steal Like an Artist Journal: A Notebook for Creative Kleptomaniacs*. New York: Workman, 2015.

Knisley, Lucy. *An Age of License*. Seattle, WA: Fantagraphics, 2014.

———. *Displacement: A Travelogue*. Seattle, WA: Fantagraphics, 2015.

———. *French Milk*. New York: Simon & Schuster, 2009.

———. *Relish: My Life in the Kitchen*. New York: FirstSecond, 2013.

———. *Something New: Tales from a Makeshift Bride*. New York: FirstSecond, 2016.

Krakauer, Jon. *Missoula: Rape and the Justice System in a College Town*. New York: Doubleday, 2015.

Kuklin, Susan. *Beyond Magenta: Transgender Teens Speak Out*. Somerville, MA: Candlewick, 2014.

LaCour, Nina. *The Disenchantments*. New York: Dutton Books, 2012.

———. *Everything Leads to You*. New York: Dutton Books, 2014.

Lamott, Anne. *Operating Instructions: A Journal of My Son's First Year*. New York: Pantheon, 1993.

Levine, Judith. *Not Buying It: My Year without Shopping*. New York: Free Press, 2006.

Lewis, C. S. *A Grief Observed*. San Francisco: HarperOne, 2001.

Lewis, John, Andrew Aydin, and Nate Powell. *March: Book One*. Marietta, GA: Top Shelf Productions, 2013.

Lewis, Sara. *The Rise: Creativity, the Gift of Failure, and the Search for Mastery*. New York: Simon & Schuster, 2014.

Lord, Karen. *The Best of All Possible Worlds*. New York: Random House, 2014.

Losse, Katherine. *The Boy Kings: A Journey into the Heart of the Social Network*. New York: Free Press, 2012.

Maitland, Sara. *A Book of Silence*. Berkeley, CA: Counterpoint, 2009.

Mandel, Emily St. John. *Station Eleven*. New York: Alfred A. Knopf, 2014.

Mantel, Hilary. *Giving Up the Ghost: A Memoir*. New York: Henry Holt, 2003.

Marshall, Paule. *Brown Girl, Brownstones*. Mineola, NY: Dover, 2009.

Martin, Jynne Dilling. *We Mammals in Hospitable Times*. Pittsburgh, PA: Carnegie Mellon University Press, 2015.

Martin, Sasha. *Life from Scratch: A Memoir of Food, Family, Forgiveness*. Washington, DC: National Geographic Society, 2015.

Maso, Carole. *The Room Lit by Roses: A Journal of Pregnancy and Birth*. Washington, DC: Counterpoint, 2000.

Maushart, Susan. *The Winter of Our Disconnect*. New York: Penguin, 2010.

McCloud, Scott. *Understanding Comics: The Invisible Art*. Northampton, MA: Tundra Publishers, 1993.

Meriweather, Louse. *Daddy Was a Number Runner*. Englewood Cliffs, NJ: Prentice-Hall, 1970.

Mezrich, Ben. *The Accidental Billionaires: The Founding of Facebook*. New York: Anchor Books, 2010.

Montgomery, L. M. *Anne of Green Gables*. Philadelphia, PA: Courage Books, 1993.

Morgan, Ann. *The World Between Two Covers: Reading the Globe*. New York: Liverright, 2015.

Nabokov, Vladimir. *Lolita*. New York: Vintage Books, 1989.

Nafisi, Azar. *Reading Lolita in Tehran: A Memoir in Books*. New York: Random House, 2003.

Notestine, Patrick. *Paramedic to the Prince: An American Paramedic's Account of Life Inside the Mysterious World of the Kingdom of Saudi Arabia*. North Charleston, SC: BookSurge Publishing, 2009.

Nutt, Amy Ellis. *Becoming Nicole: The Transformation of an American Family*. New York: Random House, 2015.

Okparanta, Chinelo. *Under the Udala Trees*. New York: Houghton Mifflin, 2015.

Okrant, Robyn. *Living Oprah: My One-Year Experiment to Walk the Walk of the Queen of Talk*. New York: Center Street, 2009.

Oliver, Mary. *Felicity: Poems*. New York: Penguin Press, 2015.

———. *Long Life*. Boston: DeCapo Press, 2005.

———. *New and Selected Poems: Volume 1*. Boston: Beacon Press, 2004.

O'Rourke, Meghan. *The Long Goodbye*. New York: Riverhead, 2011.

Orwell, George. *Animal Farm*. London: Penguin Modern Classics, 2000.

Ostlund, Lori. *After the Parade*. New York: Scribner, 2015.

Paschen, Elise and Rebekah Presson Mosby, eds. *Poetry Speaks Expanded: Hear Poets Read from Their Own Work from Tennyson to Plath*. Naperville, IL: Sourcebooks, 2007.

Potok, Chaim. *The Chosen*. New York: Ballantine, 2003.

Prince, Althea. *The Politics of Black Women's Hair*. Tyne and Wear: Idiomatic, 2010.

Pym, Barbara. *Excellent Women*. New York: Plume, 1988.

———. *A Glass of Blessings*. New York: Open Road Media, 2013.

———. *Jane and Prudence*. New York: Moyer Bell, 1999.

———. *Less Than Angels*. New York: Open Road Media, 2013.

———. *Some Tame Gazelle*. New York: Open Road Media, 2013.

Rankine, Claudia. *Citizen: An American Lyric*. Minneapolis, MN: Graywolf Press, 2014.

Rhimes, Shonda. *The Year of Yes*. New York: Simon and Schuster, 2015.

Ronson, Jon. *So You've Been Publicly Shamed*. New York: Penguin, 2015.

Rowell, Rainbow. *Fangirl*. New York: St. Martin's Griffin, 2013.

Rubin, Gretchen. *The Happiness Project*. New York: Harper Collins, 2011.

Rulfo, Juan. *Pedro Páramo*. Austin, TX: University of Texas Press, 2002.

Samuelsson, Marcus. *Aquavit and the New Scandinavian Cuisine*. New York: Houghton Mifflin Harcourt, 2003.

———. *New American Table*. New York: Houghton Mifflin Harcourt, 2009.

———. *Off Duty: The Recipes I Cook at Home*. New York: Houghton Mifflin Harcourt, 2014.

———. *The Soul of a New Cuisine*. New York: Houghton Mifflin, 2006.

———. *Yes, Chef: A Memoir*. New York: Random House, 2012.

Santiago, Esmerelda. *When I Was Puerto Rican*. Reading, MA: Addison-Wesley, 1993.

Satrapi, Marjane. *The Complete Persepolis*. New York: Pantheon, 2007.

Senior, Jennifer. *All Joy and No Fun: The Paradox of Modern Parenting*. New York: Ecco, 2014.

Sheffield, Rob. *Love Is a Mixtape: Life and Loss One Song at a Time*. New York: Three Rivers Press, 2007.

Shields, Carol. *The Stone Diaries*. New York: Penguin Classics, 2008.

Shin, Kyung-Sook. *Please Look After Mom*. New York: Alfred A. Knopf, 2011.

Slaughter, Anne-Marie. *Unfinished Business: Women Men Work Family*. New York: Random House, 2015.

Shields, Carol. *The Stone Diaries*. New York: Penguin, 2008.

Smith, Amy Elizabeth. *All Roads Lead to Austen: A Yearlong Journey with Jane*. Naperville, IL: Sourcebooks, 2012.

Smith, Betty. *A Tree Grows in Brooklyn*. New York: Perennial, 1998.

Smith, Keri. *Wreck This Journal*. New York: Penguin, 2007.

Sparks, Muriel. *Loitering with Intent*. New York: New Directions, 2001.

Stevenson, Bryan. *Just Mercy: A Story of Justice and Redemption*. New York: Spiegel & Grau, 2014.

Sullivan, Faith. *The Cape Ann*. New York: Three Rivers Press, 2010.

———. *Empress of One*. Minneapolis, MN: Milkweed, 1996.

———. *Gardenias*. Minneapolis, MN: Milkweed, 2005.

———. *Good Night, Mr. Wodehouse*. Minneapolis, MN: Milkweed, 2015.

Summers, A. K. *Pregnant Butch: Nine Long Months Spent in Drag*. Berkeley, CA: Soft Skull Press, 2014.

Swift, Jonathan. *Gulliver's Travels*. New York: Penguin Classics, 2003.

Tamaki, Mariko and Jillian Tamaki. *This One Summer*. New York: First Second, 2014.

Tan, Shaun. *The Arrival*. New York: Arthur A. Levine, 2006.

Tharp, Twyla. *The Creative Habit: Learn It and Use It for Life*. New York: Simon & Schuster, 2006.

Tharps, Lori L. *Kinky Gazpacho: Life, Love, and Spain*. New York: Washington Square Press, 2008.

Turkle, Sherry. *Reclaiming Conversation: The Power of Talk in a Digital Age*. New York: Penguin, 2014.

Voltaire. *Candide*. New York: Bantam Classics, 2003.

Wasylowski, Karen V. *Darcy and Fitzwilliam: A Tale of an Officer and a Gentleman*. Naperville, IL: Sourcebooks, 2011.

Watkins, Claire Vaye. *Gold Fame Citrus*. New York: Riverhead, 2015.

Weisman, Alan. *The World without Us*. New York: St. Martin's Press, 2007.

Winton, Tim. *Cloudstreet*. New York: Picador, 2013.

Yousafzai, Malala, with Christina Lamb. *I Am Malala: The Girl Who Stood Up for Education and Was Shot by the Taliban*. New York: Back Bay Books, 2015.

ACKNOWLEDGMENTS

We would like to thank our editor, Grace Menary-Winefield, for making this second edition possible. We really appreciate her support and belief in the project.

—Jane and Elisabeth

I would like to thank my mother for her support, book recommendations, and sharp editing eye. This book was much improved by her thoughtful feedback. I've got to give a shout-out to my online reading community, the faithful "It's Monday! What Are You Reading?" kidlit crew. These teachers and librarians, voracious readers all, keep me happily reading all year long with their recommendations and reviews. Thanks to my son who brings me joy every day. Finally, I could not have completed my part of this project without the support of my husband. It's lovely to have someone who is always in my corner. Thank you, Ryan.

—Elisabeth Ellington

I would like to thank my sister-in-law, Karen Connolly, for her fantastic recommendations and her enthusiasm for both editions of *A Year of Reading*. Thanks also to my mother-in-law, Carolyn Kenny, for years of love and encouragement but especially for understanding when her jet-lagged, insomniac daughter-in-law was typing away in her living room in the middle of the night. Thanks also to my sister Frances Freimiller LaRosa for hosting me during a month where I did nothing but eat and type, and for her book recommendations. Many thanks go to Catherine Freimiller and Louis Freimiller, who, as siblings should, kept me well supplied with cheesesteaks, donuts, and burritos. Thanks also to my sister-in-law Amy Freimiller and nephew Danny Freimiller for providing much needed breaks.

Much love and gratitude to all the LaRosas: Kate, Joe, Emilie, and the fabulous William, who kept me going. I owe my introduction to the world of books to my mother, Marjorie Freimiller, whose love continues to inspire me. Finally, many, many thanks to my husband, Kevin Connolly, who can spot a weak sentence from a mile away, suggest five stronger ones in the blink of an eye, and fix even the most bizarre of computer problems calmly and quickly. If that weren't enough, his support, care, and love during my recent illness have been essential to my recovery.

-Jane Freimiller

✎ ABOUT THE AUTHORS ✎

Elisabeth Ellington earned her PhD in British literature from Brandeis University and currently teaches in the English department at Chadron State College in Chadron, Nebraska. She lives in South Dakota with her husband, son, and six cats. Visit her online at thedirigibleplum .wordpress.com or find her on Twitter @elisabethelling.

Jane Freimiller grew up in Philadelphia and graduated from Haverford College in 1987. After earning a PhD in philosophy from Boston College, she taught at a university for several years. She lives in the United Kingdom where she works in an auction house and helps to take care of a local orchard.